JAPAN
TRAVELER'S COMPANION

ROB GOSS

TUTTLE Publishing

Tokyo | Rutland, Vermont | Singapore

CONTENTS

INTRODUCING JAPAN

1 TOKYO

2 SIDETRIPS FROM TOKYO

Nagoya City Science Museum

Sensoji Temple

Nara Park

Hachimangu Shrine

INTRODUCING JAPAN

It has become something of a cliché to talk about Japan in terms of contrasts, but Japan really is a country defined by juxtapositions. For all of Japan's technological advances, not to mention the unquenchable thirst for the new and the next you see in cities like Tokyo, Japanese society is still rooted deep in tradition. Timeless and cutting edge comfortably sit side by side, as do the sacred and the cute. Japan prides itself on an appreciation of nature, yet nowhere seems safe from concrete, a vending machine or a gaudy pachinko parlor. No wonder the country can bemuse first-timers just as much as it can keep surprising old hands.

Fushimi Inari Shrine

Ginkakuji Temple

Umeda Sky Building

Traditional Restaurant

Japan

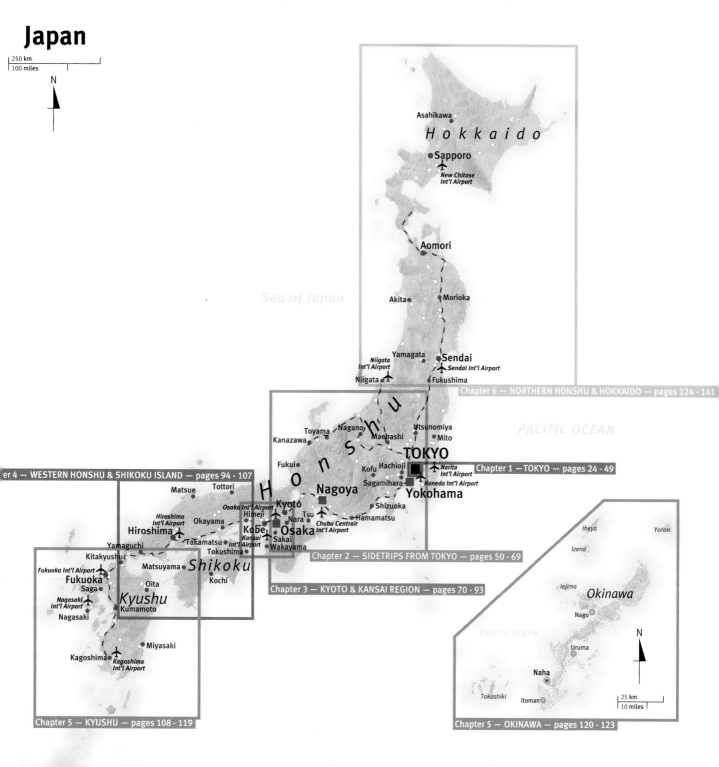

250 km
100 miles

N

Asahikawa

Hokkaido

Sapporo
New Chitose Int'l Airport

Aomori

Sea of Japan

Akita

Morioka

PACIFIC OCEAN

Yamagata
Niigata Int'l Airport
Niigata

Sendai
Sendai Int'l Airport
Fukushima

Toyama
Nagano
Kanazawa
Maebashi
Utsunomiya
Mito

Fukui

Honshu

Kofu
Hachioji
TOKYO
Narita Int'l Airport

Matsue
Tottori
Sagamihara
Haneda Int'l Airport

Nagoya
Yokohama

Osaka Int'l Airport
Kyoto
Shizuoka
Hiroshima Int'l Airport
Okayama
Himeji
Nara
Tsu
Chubu Centrair Int'l Airport
Hamamatsu

Hiroshima
Kobe
Osaka
Kansai Int'l Airport
Sakai
Takamatsu
Yamaguchi
Wakayama
Kitakyushu
Tokushima
Shikoku
Matsuyama

Fukuoka Int'l Airport
Fukuoka
Saga
Oita
Kochi

Iheya
Yoron

Nagasaki Int'l Airport
Kyushu
Kumamoto
Izena

Nagasaki

Iejima

Okinawa

PACIFIC OCEAN

Nago

Miyasaki

Kagoshima
Kagoshima Int'l Airport

Uruma

Naha

Tokashiki
Itoman

N

25 km
10 miles

A Modern Nation That Still Values its Traditional Past

Progress is unrelenting and rapier in many fields and facets of Japan, yet there's no shortage of areas where the country happily stands firm against the drifting sands of time. Just cast your eyes over a typical tourist brochure, where kimono-clad geisha shuffle between appointments in Kyoto's Gion district, Mount Fuji stands capped in white and sumo wrestlers batter each other senseless, and you'll realize that timeless is big in Japan.

For a visitor, that means getting to experience an array of cultural delights often far removed from anything back home. You can eat forms of cuisine (pages 14–17) that have been perfected over centuries. You can shop for and even try your hand at traditional crafts as diverse as pottery, indigo dyeing, and making *washi* paper. You can even go deeper with Zen meditation classes, cooking classes, ikebana flower arranging workshops, the tea ceremony and far beyond. In cities such as Tokyo, Kyoto and Osaka, you can watch highly stylized kabuki theater or check out Noh theater, geisha shows and the old-fashioned slapstick comedy of *manzai*. All over the country you can visit historic sites like the World Heritage-designated shrines and temples of Kyoto and Nara, Himeji

ABOVE Horyuji Temple in Nara (page 82), home to some of the oldest wooden buildings in the world.
LEFT A monk in Kamakura (page 56), Japan's capital from 1185–1333. The town is only an hour from central Tokyo, but retains so many reminders of its rich past that it feels like an entirely different world.
FRONT ENDPAPER Cherry blossoms at Takato Castle Ruins Park in Nagano.
TITLE PAGE The Hanagasa Odori, a local community dance in Yamagata.
PAGE 2, TOP LEFT Billboards at Kabukicho in Shinjuku.
PAGE 2, TOP RIGHT Japanese maple trees in a peaceful setting.

PAGE 2, MIDDLE RIGHT The sparrow dance, first performed to celebrate the completion of Sendai Castle.
PAGE 2, MIDDLE The biggest of Japan's eleven Pokémon Centers is in Ikebukuro, Tokyo.
PAGE 2, BOTTOM A pretty confectionery purse.
PAGE 3, TOP Some of the best things to do in Tokyo include having beer and *yakitori* chicken skewers at Omoide Yokocho (Memory Lane) (top left), enjoying awesome views from the Tokyo Metropolitan Government Building (middle left) or Tokyo Tower's observation deck (top right), and visiting the iconic Sensoji Temple (center).
PAGE 3, MIDDLE Taking a rickshaw ride could be a fun way to see the sights.

Castle, and many other places that leave an indelible imprint on travelers.

Along with all that tradition also comes formality. Japanese has a complex system of formal honorific speech for use in certain business and social settings to show respect, highlight status and so on. Behavior is formalized, too. The Japanese don't go around bowing deeply to everyone all the time (life doesn't mimic most travel documentaries), but there are set patterns of behavior for many situations, whether that's how business cards are exchanged (given and received with both hands) or how a potential customer is greeted when they enter a store.

Remove the tourist brochure sugar coating and at times Japan's fondness for

ABOVE AND LEFT Kyoto's Gion Matsuri is one of Japan's biggest annual events. Lasting throughout July and featuring events that include a massive procession of floats through central Kyoto, the festival began in the 800s as a purification ritual to ward off a plague.

LEFT Be it Kyoto's temple gardens or classic stroll gardens in Tokyo such as Kiyosumi and Rikugien, traditional landscaping is another aspect of old Japan that thankfully shows no sign of moving aside.

ABOVE A display of archery in Tokyo's Meiji Shrine. Japan is a very forward-looking country in many regards, but there is still a strong appreciation of (and pride in) its samurai past. You see that in so many places, from reenactments and even to Japan's national football team—nicknamed "Samurai Blue".

tradition can be a negative, too; although for a foreigner the negatives often manifest themselves as humorous and quaint rather than an annoyance. Starting with the annoying, in many companies, business can progress slowly, with decision-making processes rarely deviating from cumbersome time-honored patterns. It doesn't matter if a policy or procedure is inefficient, change would be worse— better the devil you know than the devil you don't. Avoid risk at all cost. Stick to the rules, at least publicly (one must keep face, after all), no matter how silly they seem. With that, Japan has "No" signs everywhere, from funny cartoon manner posters on the trains to warning signs in toilets (albeit not enough signs that tell elderly locals to stop spitting in the street!). Yet even the long list of "Nos" in places like hotels isn't intended to be unwelcoming, it's all about avoiding conflict and disruption; about keeping the *wa* (harmony). And in Japan, there's nothing quite as timeless as that.

ABOVE One of the small gardens at Daitokuji Temple in Kyoto.
BELOW Ritsurin Garden in Takamatsu on Shikoku, the smallest of Japan's four main islands, is an expansive example of traditional landscaping that utilizes the concept of borrowed scenery—incorporating the natural surrounds around the garden as a backdrop to its actual design.

ABOVE Images of geisha and *maiko* (trainee geisha) in Kyoto might be considered a touch clichéd by some, but there's nothing fake about the glimpses of geisha you might well get to enjoy in the former capital.

ABOVE Magome, one of the beautifully preserved towns along the old Nakasendo highway that connected Edo and Kyoto.

ABOVE Weddings for some are still a traditional Shinto affair, although white weddings are far more common.

BELOW The stunning Himeji Castle.

ABOVE Green tea doesn't have to be part of a ceremony. For many, it's a simple, daily staple much like coffee.

Hi-Tech Design and an Obsessive Attention to Small Details

Visit any part of urban Japan and the country's modern faces don't so much reveal themselves, they pounce. For a first-time visit, it can be a dizzying experience. Concrete dominates. Cities increasingly grow upwards from their centers, and then roll long and flat unbroken far beyond their arbitrary borders. They are frequently crowded, too, from cramped train carriages and crawling highways to heaving shopping malls. Vending machines are on every corner; convenience stores, too. It's energetic, often chaotic, but never dull. And while sometimes it feels like Japan refuses to cut its umbilical cord to the Edo era (try dealing with a Japanese bank or, far more seriously, look at something like the lack of gender equality) there are times when it feels the country has gone further into the future than Buck Rogers.

Architecture is certainly one area where Japan continuously pushes the boundaries, and the gray of central Tokyo in particular is often punctuated by the cutting-edge work of internationally acclaimed Japanese architects like Toyo Ito,

ABOVE The E5 Series is one of the newer bullet trains, debuting in 2011 and with a maximum speed of 320 km/h (200 mph).
TOP A Kawasaki prototype. Japan's automotive companies frequently lead the way.
LEFT Nagoya City Science Museum. As well as the futuristic design, inside it's full of hands-on activities designed to inspire the next generation of scientists.

Tadao Ando, Shigeru Ban, Kisho Kurokawa, and Kenzo Tange. Pritzker Prize-winning Ando's Omotesando Hills is an obvious example of modern Japanese style, although the former boxer, former trucker's (and self-taught architect's) work in Naoshima (pages 102–103) is arguably more representative of his distinctive use of rough concrete, stark spaces, and natural lighting.

Then there's technology and manufacturing. With automotives, names like Nissan, Honda, Suzuki, Daihatsu, Mazda, and Toyota—the latter whose factory tours are a highlight of a trip to Nagoya—have made Japan one of a small group of global leaders, as, a little less fashionably, have industrial and heavy machine makers such as Mitsubishi. It's similar within home electronics and brands

ABOVE A prototype on display at Toyota's main production complex near Nagoya. A visit here can also include a tour of the high-tech, mostly automated production lines.
TOP LEFT The Tokyo Big Sight convention center in Tokyo's Odaiba district.
LEFT It might look like something from *Thunderbirds*, but this is one of the boats that transports people up and down the Sumida River, running from Asakusa to Hamarikyu Gardens and Odaiba.

LEFT Toyota's companion robot Kirobo Mini, who has traveled to the International Space Station.
BELOW LEFT One of Toyota's robots. Now it just plays the violin for school kids, but one day developers hope robots will be able to function as care-givers, concierges and in many other capacities.
RIGHT The Shinjuku skyline.
BELOW Naoshima is home to dozens of art installations, such as the *Frog and Cat* by Karel Appel pictured here, as well as several museums.

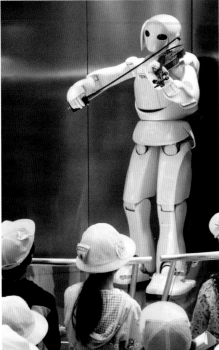

such as Panasonic, Sony, NEC, and Hitachi. And don't forget the cameras of Nikon, Canon, Fuji, Minolta, and more. Yet, back to the contrasts, even in a country where robots greet customers with a bow, bathtubs talk and toilets perform a wash and dry, sometimes even the simplest and most effective low-tech solutions are overlooked—just try and find a flat with good insulation.

Beyond that, Japan is also a leader when it comes to things geeky. For gamers, think PlayStation and Nintendo. For cartoons, comic and animation, where to start? It permeates all parts of Japanese society. You see adults reading thick manga comics on rush hour trains. All sorts of companies, from tourism agencies to shrines, use comic strips and mascots to get their messages across. And Japanese manga and anime have legions of fans around the globe, in the process spawning a billion-dollar business.

ABOVE AND RIGHT Japan's *otaku*, which could roughly translate as geek (although that doesn't quite capture all the nuances), fuel massive anime, manga and related industries. From cosplay outfits to figurines, video games to comics, visit Akihabara in Tokyo and you can take in all of Japan's *otaku* color and energy.

ABOVE A "game center" (amusement arcade). In Tokyo and elsewhere, they come in all shapes and sizes, from virtual reality-heavy centers like Joypolis to old-school, retro-only arcades where you can turn back the clock with a bit of *Street Fighter*.

RIGHT Depending on one's point of view, the Robot Restaurant in Shinjuku's glitzy, neon-heavy multimedia cabaret could be the ultimate in tacky or wonderful kitsch.

A Foodie's Paradise

Food. Be it sushi, ramen or any of the hundreds of other dishes found around Japan, Japanese cuisine has to be one of the country's greatest claims to fame. In a nation full of foodies, food is a central fixture of celebrations and festivals, food-related shows dominate prime time TV, cookbooks and cooking magazines fill entire aisles in bookstores, and wherever you go it rarely feels you are that far from somewhere to grab a bite to eat. Tokyo alone is home to somewhere near 100,000 licensed eating establishments that range from almost three hundred wallet-busting Michelin-starred restaurants to simple, standing-only noodle joints that give change from ¥500. Leave aside the vast selection of international flavors, the varieties of just Japanese cuisine are mind blowing, but despite that variety there are certain threads that bind everything together.

A focus on the use of seasonal produce is shared by many types of Japanese cuisine, from the in-season vegetables in Buddhist *shojin ryori* cuisine to the seafood selected by sushi restaurants. So is specialization: restaurants dedicated only to soba noodles, tofu dishes, pork cutlets, tempura, and many other single foods are extremely common. Look at Tokyo and you'll see that certain areas specialize, too. Okubo, a part of Shinjuku, is home to a concentration of Korean restaurants. Ryogoku is known for *chanko nabe*, the hot pot of meat, vegetables and seafood used by sumo wrestlers to bulk up. The Tsukishima area is the birthplace of *monjayaki*, a happy-tasting but not especially appetizing-looking dish that

LEFT AND ABOVE Street food stalls selling *takoyaki*—battered chunks of octopus that get lathered in a gooey soy-based sauce and mayo, and then topped with fish flakes.

TOP *Kaiseki ryori*, the ultimate in Japanese cuisine. You can drop several hundred dollars per person at the best *kaiseki* restaurants, but good versions can be found much cheaper as part of a stay in a traditional Japanese ryokan.

RIGHT Pickles on display at Kyoto's Nishiki Market, a must-stop on any foodie's trip to Kyoto. MIDDLE Tofu comes in many different textures and is served in a variety of ways. Try it as part of a *shojin ryori* vegetarian meal and you'll very possibly shed any notion of it being the dull health food it's too often considered in the West.

RIGHT *Okonomiyaki*, the savory pancake-like dish that's found all over but is a specialty in Osaka and Hiroshima. A mix of diced cabbage, batter, eggs and anything else you might want to add (pork and kimchi is a great option!), diners cook it themselves on hotplates built into the table.

begins as a runny batter containing chopped vegetables, meat or seafood and then after a while on a hotplate becomes a sticky mess like fried cheese.

And this kind of specializing stretches out on a national scale, too. Almost every region, city and even small town you visit will have at least one local dish it is proud of. Moving away from Tokyo, Yokohama has its Chinatown restaurants. Up north in Hokkaido, the harsh, cold climate has given Sapporo local specialties that include warming soup curry (like a mulligatawny), a hearty miso-based version of ramen, and a type of mutton barbecue somewhat oddly named after Genghis Khan. At the opposite end of the archipelago, balmy Okinawa has a version of soba noodles in broth that are topped with melt-in-the-mouth pork (*soki soba*), a wonderful stir-fry of bitter gourd,

ABOVE A *teppanyaki* restaurant, where the chefs display expert knife skills and flair in cooking the meat, seafood and vegetables in front of you.

spam, tofu and egg called *goya champuru*, and oddities that include vinegared pig's ears (*mimiga*) and stewed pig's trotters (*tonsoku*). And where to start with Kyoto? You can find restaurants serving refined *kaiseki* cuisine all over the country, but the multi-course collection of artistically presented seasonal delicacies is never better than in Kyoto.

In fact, play a word association game with a Japanese friend, and you'll likely get a lot of foodie responses. Osaka? *Okonomiyaki* (a kind of savory pancake) and *takoyaki* (battered chunks of octopus). Niigata? The *koshihikari* rice variety. Kyushu? Hakata ramen. Shikoku? Udon noodles and oranges. The list could go on and on, but the takeaway is simple: very little is more important than food in Japan.

ABOVE Check out the lanterns outside an izakaya and they often tell you what kind of food is inside to go with the beer and sake. This one advertises *kushikatsu* (deep-fried skewered meat) and *yakisoba* (fried noodles) among other things.

LEFT Sushi is the most famous of Japanese foods. You could easily drop $300 at a top sushi restaurant in somewhere like Ginza or you could binge on a budget at a revolving train sushi bar (*kaitenzushi*). Even the cheapest options tend to be good, even if it's a ¥500 supermarket sushi bento.

LEFT Thanks to some stellar marketing Kobe beef gets all the plaudits overseas, but in Japan it's just one of dozens of highly rated wagyu beef brands. Aficionados tend to rate *Kobe-gyu*, *Matsuzaka-gyu* (Mie Prefecture) and *Ohmi-gyu* (Shiga Prefecture) as the top three, but also look out for *Yonezawa-gyu*, *Hitachi-gyu*, and *Kyoto-gyu* amongst others.

BELOW Ramen is cheap, ubiquitous and much loved. There are numerous regional variations, too, from the miso-based Sapporo ramen to the pork bone broth-based Hakata ramen. Regardless of variety, a quick way to tell if a place is good or not—the length of the queue.

BELOW *Yakitori* (grilled chicken on skewers) is one of those Japanese foods that can be pricey or cheap, served in plush surrounds or chargrilled in backstreet stalls. Either way, it's a must-try.

RIGHT Even the cheapest of soba noodle stands are worth a try. For as little as ¥300, you can get a hot bowl of noodles topped with a veggie tempura—perfect for a quick bite on the go, which is why you'll often find them in and around stations, sometimes standing only.

A Panoply of Extraordinary Festivals and Celebrations

Japan's myriad festivals mark the changing of seasons and rites of passage, they light up summer skies and add moments of warmth to harsh winters, bring communities together and keep traditions alive. They are so deeply interwoven into Japanese society that whatever time of year you might visit Japan and whichever part of the country you find yourself in, there's a strong chance that a festival (or *matsuri* to use the Japanese word) of some kind or other will be taking place nearby.

Come to Japan in spring and the most obvious events will be the cherry-blossom parties (called *hanami*; literally, "flower viewing") that follow the annual wave of *sakura* (cherry blossom) northward across the country, with the whole of Japan seemingly welcoming spring with picnics and parties under the delicate pink blossoms. With blossoms soon turning brown on the ground and spring starting to give way to summer, the number of festivals increases. To pluck out a few of the annual highlights, there's the Sanja Matsuri in May in Tokyo's Asakusa, where amid huge crowds frenzied groups of bearers carry highly decorative portable shrines through streets in honor of the seventh-century founders of Sensoji Temple. Or for a couple more with deep historical roots, there's the Gion Matsuri in Kyoto in July with its processions of floats and people in period dress, and in the sweltering heat of mid-August Tokushima's Awa Odori, which sees dance troupes clad in colorful traditional costumes prance and shout day and night to a pulsating accompaniment of *shamisen*, flute, bells and drums, attracting in excess of a million visitors to the city over three days.

BELOW The Jidai Matsuri in October sees Kyoto turn the clock back with processions in period costumes.
BELOW RIGHT The Aoi Matsuri in Kyoto sees decorated *furyugasa* umbrellas being paraded.

LEFT Visit Japan in late March or early April for the best Japanese celebration of them all: *hanami* (cherry blossom viewing). The pink blossoms only stay for a couple of weeks, with their spectacular peak lasting just days, but send Japan into a frenzy of celebrations.

RIGHT Japan also welcomes events from other cultures, such as the annual Asakusa Samba Festival.

RIGHT The Yayoi Festival celebrated in April in Nikko. Dating to the late 700s, the annual event welcomes in spring, with the highlight being a parade of eleven of these decorative floats.

BELOW LEFT Watch a sumo tournament when in Japan if you can. There are six taking place every odd month of the year. The most expensive (and possibly most dangerous) are the ringside seats, where wrestlers may collide into the spectators.

BELOW It doesn't really matter what the occasion—Coming of Age Day in January or a summer fireworks display—you see people in colorful kimono or *yukata* at many of Japan's festivals.

More than anything, however, across Japan high summer is fireworks season, with events like Tokyo's Sumida River Fireworks Festival illuminating the sky and bringing the streets to life with a mixture of colorful street stalls selling festival staples like *yakisoba* (fried noodles), *yakitori* (chicken skewers) and *kakigori* (shaved ice), not to mention the brightly patterned cotton *yukata* summer kimono worn by many of the onlookers.

In autumn, some of the best festivals are connected to major shrines, with traditional parades and displays of horseback archery taking place in Kamakura and Nikko as part of Tsurugaoka Hachimangu Shrine's and Toshogu Shrine's seasonal celebrations. Then comes winter, when almost the entire nation welcomes in the new year with shrine visits and the northern regions come in to their own with snow and ice festivals, the most famous of which sees Sapporo in Hokkaido (page 132) transformed into an outdoor gallery of giant ice sculptures at the Snow Festival in February. And with that we've only just touched tip of the *matsuri* iceberg.

LEFT A monk walks on coals at the Fire-Walking Festival in Miyajima. Similar events are held around Japan, including a major one on Mount Takao in Tokyo on the second Sunday of March where onlookers can walk the coals themselves.
BELOW A spring festival at Daigoji Temple in Kyoto celebrates cherry blossom season and commemorates shogun Toyotomi Hideyoshi, who had seven hundred cherry blossom trees planted here in the late 1500s.
RIGHT The Oniyarai Shinji Festival is part of the annual *setsubun* festivities that mark winter's end. To ward off evil and welcome in good, people throw beans at demons, shouting "*Oni wa soto*" (Demons out!).

An Unforgettable Night at a Traditional Inn or Hot Spring

More than simply places to sleep or bases from which to explore, Japan's traditional forms of accommodation represent a chance to go deeper into Japan's multiple cultural layers.

RIGHT AND OPPOSITE TOP RIGHT Soaking in a piping-hot *onsen* (hot-spring bath) is one of the key attractions at most ryokan. Many ryokan will have a mix of indoor and outdoor gender-separated baths (although some still have mixed gender), where the mineral-rich water is said to alleviate not just fatigue but many other ailments. To bath correctly, you just need to remember a few rules: wash and rinse thoroughly by the low showers before getting in the communal water, and make sure you are completely naked.

ABOVE AND RIGHT Dining at a ryokan is a special experience in and of itself. Taking a couple of hours, the *kaiseki* dinner generally features beautifully presented dish after dish · that utilize regional and seasonal produce. Breakfast, too, can be a big affair, combining rice, fish, pickles, eggs, soup, salad, and plenty more.

Take the ryokan, the traditional Japanese inn, which ranges from modest, family-run affairs to refined five-star luxury, but at its heart shares several core traits. Firstly, a typical stay here means a night sleeping on a futon in a tatami-mat room furnished with low table and defined by traditional design elements that include paper screen doors and calligraphy wall hangings. Then there is the food, usually a stomach-busting multi-dish breakfast that includes rice, fish, pickles and soup, but more importantly a multi-course dinner based around seasonal local produce that's served on fine ceramics and lacquerware like a succession of miniature art works. On top of that, most ryokan also feature communal *onsen* (hot spring baths), sometimes inside, sometimes out, sometimes both, which add a soothing touch of pampering. All that, of course, would merely be window dressing if it weren't for the level of hospitality and attentive service that usually comes with it—although despite rose-tinted reputation, it has to be said that Japan can do

ABOVE Ryokan come in a variety of styles, from swanky contemporary to former samurai houses, but this is the classic guest-room design—a mix of tatami, low table, paper screen doors and views out to nature.

inhospitable and poor service, too, especially if you run into someone who behind the smile is terrified of or just plain dislikes foreigners!

Away from the ryokan come variations on the theme. *Minshuku* are a homely version of ryokan (like a B&B), without the formal level of service that comes with a ryokan, but in many respects even warmer for it. Then *shukubo* offer another twist, this time provided on temple grounds and typically being a more Spartan version of a ryokan, with the vegetarian cuisine eaten by monks on the menu and service functional but friendly. Better yet, *shukubo* offer opportunities to get a deeper look at spiritual Japan, not just by staying in the tranquil surrounds of a temple, but by being able to observe and take part in the temple's morning rituals.

ABOVE *Okami* is the term given to the proprietress or manageress of a ryokan. She will be there to greet you upon arrival, and she oversees the staff as they look after you during your stay. In smaller ryokan, she might even be more hands-on, helping to serve the lavish multi-course meals in your room.

CHAPTER 1
TOKYO

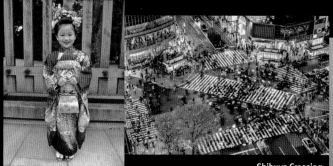

Dressed up for the 7-5-3 festival

Shibuya Crossing

Tokyo Skytree

Shibuya on Halloween

INTRODUCING TOKYO

Unlike historic Kyoto and Nara, Tokyo only came to prominence in the early 1600s. Then, just little more than a village named Edo, shogun Tokugawa Ieyasu chose to turn the modest fortifications overlooking Edo into a mighty castle from where he would rule his newly unified country. From there, the de facto capital boomed, and by the time of the Meiji Restoration of 1868—when Edo officially took Kyoto's place as capital, and had its name changed to Tokyo (the Eastern Capital)—the village had transformed into a city of 600,000. It's not looked back. Today Tokyo is home to almost fourteen million, a number that swells to more than thirty-five million if you include the parts of neighboring prefectures that make up the Greater Tokyo area. With that there are no surprises when it comes to Tokyo's energy, its crowds, and its color, but they are just a few parts of a metropolis that mixes touches of the old with swathes of the ultra-modern.

Harajuku Cosplayers

Sensoji Temple

Imperial Palace

Meiji Shrine

Tokyo's Bustling Central Districts

For generations Ginza has signified Tokyo at its most exclusive. Just drop the name and for many Japanese it will conjure up images of fine dining, plush department stores and boutiques, not to mention the exorbitantly priced hostess clubs that boomed in the 1980s bubble. That's not a new thing; the area's connection to wealth goes well beyond recent memory. In its earliest Edo-era days, Ginza was home to a silver mint (*gin za,* hence the area's name) created by the first Edo shogun, Tokugawa Ieyasu, the man who united a war-torn Japan at the turn of the seventeenth century and, with Tokyo (then called Edo) as his new capital, initiated an (almost) isolationist dynasty that would last until the Meiji Restoration of the 1860s.

In the Meiji era, Ginza was at the forefront of Tokyo's Western-influenced development. With the support of European architects, the district saw its fire-prone wooden buildings replaced by stone architecture, its muddy streets transformed into paved roads, and eventually the advent of electric trams and subways. Head to the Ginza Crossing today and you can still see examples of that early architecture in the shape of the Wako

LEFT AND BELOW Whether neon-drenched at night or glistening in the sunshine, Ginza always manages to retain a flashy sense of high style.

MIDDLE LEFT Ginza teems with architecturally striking flagship stores for high-end brands like Bulgari, Cartier, Chanel, Mikimoto and many others.

department store, whose curved granite façade and clock tower (first built in 1894, but then redone shortly after the 1923 Great Kanto Earthquake) stand across from another landmark in the prestigious 1930-built Mitsukoshi department store.

Today, shopping is one of the major draws to Ginza. Along with Mitsukoshi and Wako, you have branches of Matsuya and Printemps department stores, the plush Ginza 6 shopping complex, a slew of sleekly designed flagships for European luxury brands like Bulgari, Cartier, Chanel, and Omega (to call out just a handful) and—highlighting the trend toward simple,

OPPOSITE PAGE The Wako department store at the Ginza Crossing.
RIGHT It's not just expensive brands and boutiques in Ginza nowadays. Simple, affordable and extremely popular stores like Uniqlo and Muji are going from strength to strength in Japan, Ginza included.

"un-branded" fashions—major local branches of local retailers Muji and Uniqlo. Then, of course, comes the food. It isn't all in the wallet-hurting category, but the fact that thirty-eight restaurants in Ginza have Michelin stars speaks volumes. If you wanted to splurge on the best sushi, finest tempura or most expensive wagyu steak, Ginza would be the place to do it. Yet on the flipside, if you wanted something cheaper, the restaurants under the elevated train tracks that cut between Ginza and the Imperial Palace area have the cheerful side of Japanese cuisine with *yakitori* joints, izakaya and plenty of other casual places.

And what of the Imperial Palace area? Heading there from the Marunouchi side of Tokyo Station you get a real clash of the old and the new, the station's restored historic 1914 façade dwarfed by the skyscrapers of the Marunouchi business district, shimmering giants that appeared during Marunouchi's much needed facelift of the early 2000s and which on the opposite side to the station now cast their reflections in the outer moats of the palace grounds. Beyond some simple but unspectacular gardens, there isn't really all that much to explore at the palace—although the uninterrupted three-mile (five-kilometer) running loop around it is one of the best runs in Tokyo—but that doesn't stop busloads upon busloads of visitors from coming to snap photos of the

ABOVE The Marunouchi area on the Imperial Palace side of Tokyo Station. Over the past decade, the neighborhood has been transformed by multipurpose skyscrapers like the Marunouchi Building—it's not just gray offices here anymore, but swanky bars, restaurants, shops, and hotels.
RIGHT The old Tokyo Station building has recently undergone a renovation and is well worth exploring to view its early twentieth-century interior.
BELOW Ginza isn't just about Michelin restaurants. In the neighboring Shimbashi and Yurakucho areas are hundreds of lively, value restaurants and bars popular for unwinding after work.
OPPOSITE PAGE FAR RIGHT The Nijubashi Bridge and an outer turret at Tokyo's Imperial Palace.
OPPOSITE PAGE TOP LEFT AND RIGHT Ginza is home to some of the city's finest and most exclusive sushi restaurants, but the freshest can be found at Tsukiji Market, southeast of Ginza.

THE TSUKIJI FISH MARKET

Will it or won't it? As of the time this was written—and very likely when you are reading it, too—the future of Japan's largest market and one of Tokyo's finest foodie destinations is up in the air. In November 2016, large parts of Tsukiji Market, a twenty-minute walk southeast of Ginza, should have begun relocating to a new site in nearby Toyosu, but a soil contamination scandal at the new (and fully built) market has put that in doubt. How long it will be delayed or whether the relocation will even be canceled, nobody seems to know for sure, but the upshot is this—you might still be able to visit Tsukiji. The early-morning tuna auctions here are worth a 4am alarm just by themselves, but mix that with a walk around the multiple warehouses and inner and market areas, where some sixty thousand wholesalers, buyers and shippers trade two thousand tons of seafood and other produce daily and you get to experience one of Tokyo's most colorful and energetic spots. Even better, the sushi and other seafood breakfasts available at the many restaurants in and around the market don't come any fresher.

moats and the few off-limits structures that are visible. And to be fair, as Tokyo goes, the classic palace photo—the doubled-arched Nijubashi Bridge in the foreground with an Edo-era guard tower poking through thick woods beyond the moat behind—is undoubtedly one of Tokyo's most iconic historic sights.

Glimpses of Tokyo Old and New

Asakusa and its neighboring areas form the heart of Tokyo's *shitamachi* (literally "low town")—the city's traditional working-class east side—and are the perfect counterpoint to the sleek and chic parts of central Tokyo. Forget European boutiques and cosmopolitan malls, swanky cafés and hipster fashion—this is the real Tokyo; friendly, chatty, sometimes a bit rough around the edges, full of color and packed with history.

Looking back at the history of Asakusa, the area grew up around what is still its most famous sight, Sensoji, a temple that legend has it was founded in the early 600s to house a statue of Kannon, the goddess of mercy, fished out of the nearby Sumida River by two brothers. While Sensoji has gone through numerous incarnations since (that happens in a disaster-prone city like Tokyo), its current look comfortably makes it Tokyo's standout temple. Smack in the

RIGHT New and old merge in Asakusa's skyline, with Sensoji Temple's ancient five-level pagoda and the spanking new Tokyo Skytree tower.

ABOVE Girls in patterned kimono in front of the Hozomon Gate and its iconic red lantern.
LEFT Nakamise-dori is the street that runs between Sensoji Temple's two towering gates, delivering a colorful mix of touristy souvenirs, moreish snacks and the occasional local craft.

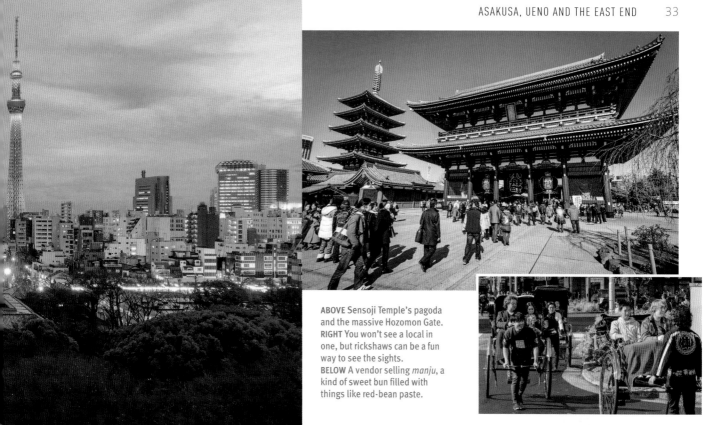

ABOVE Sensoji Temple's pagoda and the massive Hozomon Gate.
RIGHT You won't see a local in one, but rickshaws can be a fun way to see the sights.
BELOW A vendor selling *manju*, a kind of sweet bun filled with things like red-bean paste.

middle of Tokyo's far-from-glitzy east-end urban sprawl, the 39-foot (12-meter) high, 39-foot wide Kaminarimon roofed gateway to the complex is in stark contrast to its surroundings, although that's only the start of things. What follows is a colorful stall-lined street that leads onto the even more imposing, 72-foot (22-meter) high Hozomon Gate, which then gives way to Sensoji's five-story pagoda and main hall. It's frequently crowded with tourists and all the touristy touches that come with that (rickshaw rides included), but nevertheless it's an incredible complex.

Away from Sensoji, a walk around Asakusa also provides a glimpse at the area's pre-World War Two position as Tokyo's main entertainment district, with places like the rickety, retro and tiny Hanayashiki amusement park, which once was one of Tokyo's major draws because of its now sedate-feeling roller coaster (the first in Japan in 1953). Then there's Rokku Broadway, a street traditionally known for its theaters, like Engei Hall, the place to catch classic *shitamachi* comic storytelling such as *rakugo* and slapstick *manzai* standup acts. For street food, spilling out onto the backstreets around here are also some of Tokyo's most welcoming and cheap-and-cheerful *yakitori* (chargrilled chicken) restaurants.

LEFT Tokyo National Museum.
BELOW Ueno Park is one of Tokyo's most popular cherry blossom party spots.

BELOW Ameya Yokocho Market, commonly called Ameyoko, began as an army-surplus flea market during the postwar American occupation.

A couple of stations north of Asakusa is Ueno, another vibrant *shitamachi* district. In spring, Ueno Park is one of the liveliest places in Japan to take in the annual front of pink cherry blossoms, with picnickers and partiers filling the park from morning to night during the blossoms' fleeting visit. Besides that, alongside a zoo (if that's your thing), Toshogu shrine, and a lily-covered lake around which food stalls often set up, Ueno boasts an impressive collection of museums, including the magnificent collection at Tokyo National Museum, which covers everything from priceless seventh-and eighth-century artifacts from Horyuji Temple in Nara to armor, ceramics, screen paintings, and tea utensils. Quite different in its focus, another museum well worth the admission is the Shitamachi Museum, which brings old Tokyo to life with exhibits that include a reconstruction of a cramped 1920s tenement row. In the now, the *shitamachi* vibe in Ueno is best felt in and around the Ameya Yokocho Market, a long street full of fish and vegetable stalls, budget clothing and accessories, teas and dried foods, which starts across the road from Ueno Station and follows the elevated train lines, merging and connecting with more backstreets that reveal a slew of cheap eateries and *tachinomiya* (standing bars)—the perfect place to grab a bite and a drink and mix with normal Tokyoites.

Look east over the Sumida River from Asakusa and you get to see one of Tokyo's most distinctive views; the combination of the 2,080-foot (634-meter) Tokyo Skytree tower, the world's second tallest structure when finished in 2012, and the older head offices of Asahi Breweries, where one building is designed to look like a frothy glass of beer and the other has odd-looking "flames" built onto it that have

earned it the unfortunate nickname *unchi biru* (turd building). From this part of Asakusa, you can also get a different view of Tokyo with a boat trip, heading down the Sumida River to the Hamarikyu Gardens or nearby Tsukiji Market (page 31) or further to Odaiba.

On the way south the boat passes (but doesn't stop at) Ryogoku, home to Japan's main sumo stadium, the Kokugikan, which hosts three fifteen-day tournaments annually (in January, May and September). This being the center of Japan's sumo world, you'll also find many sumo stables here and in neighboring areas (some of which can be visited as parts of organized tours), as well as numerous restaurants specializing in *chanko nabe*, the substantial hot pot eaten by sumo wrestlers to maintain their famous bulk.

ABOVE *Chanko nabe*, consisting of a *dashi* or chicken-broth soup base, large amounts of protein and served with rice, is a staple food eaten by sumo wrestlers.
RIGHT Top-ranked sumo wrestlers parade on the *dohyo* (ring) prior to the day's main bouts. You can get tickets for as little as ¥2,260 for what is a very unique spectacle.

ABOVE Tokyo Skytree and one of Tokyo's oddest buildings, the Philippe Starck-designed offices for the beer brewer Asahi. As well as being part of a complex that includes restaurants, shops and even an aquarium, the Skytree's observation decks provide by far the best panoramic views of Tokyo.

Tokyo's Geekiest Neighborhood

Akihabara in northeast Tokyo is geek land—a home for cosplayers, comic fans, anime lovers, Godzilla figurine collectors, retro arcade game addicts, and many others who proudly call themselves *otaku*. In one word, you can call it colorful. With a few more words—add techy, vibrant and frequently bizarre.

Akiba, as it's known for short, started to attract *otaku* (geeks) in the late 1980s as part of the video game boom, and gaming is still big in the area, with a mix of retro and high-tech "game centers" (arcades) as well as stores like Retro Game Camp and Traders that have every conceivable kind of PC and console game available. Then came the anime and manga. Most obviously you can see this out in the streets, where it's common to see *otaku* cosplayers dressed up as their favorite characters from anime, manga or video games—but that's just the tip of the iceberg. Start window shopping along Akiba's main street, Chuo-dori, and it's soon obvious just how *otaku*-saturated Akiba has become, not just with popular anime and manga stores like Animate and Mandrake, but with places like the multi-floor Don Quixote, Gee Store Akiba and plenty of other smaller shops selling cosplay outfits, model kits, trading cards, and all manner of other geeky gear. And no conversation about *otaku* can forget maid cafés, where young, doe-eyed waitresses in frilly French-maid outfits serve customers with huge doses of sickly sweet cuteness.

What about Akihabara before the *otaku* arrived? Then it was all about electronics, something that has its roots in post-war black-market trading of radio parts and has over the years morphed into a real mishmash of stores, from cramped backstreet electrical components and used computer stores like the numerous branches of Sofmap to robot specialists such as Tsukumo Robot Kingdom and giant home electronic megastores like Akky, Ishimaru Denki, Laox and the massive Yodobashi camera megastore on Akihabara Station's east side.

BELOW LEFT A maid from one of Akiba's maid cafés. You'll often see them in the streets advertising their stores. At work, besides serving food and drink and fawning over customers, for a small fee the maids will also play games like *janken* (rock, paper, scissors). And it's not just geared to geeky young men; women go, too—there are even butler cafés around just for them.

RIGHT AND BELOW Chuo-dori is Akihabara's main street, full of home-electronics stores, game arcades, comic shops, and other outlets aimed firmly at Japan's computer-, anime-, and manga-loving *otaku*.

ABOVE There's no escaping anime and manga in Akiba—even on the street!
BELOW Gundam Café, designed to evoke the futuristic world of one of Japan's most successful ever sci-fi media franchises, the *Gundam* series. Starting with the anime series *Mobile Suit Gundam* in 1979, it now spreads across TV, movies, video games, manga, and anime.

Tokyo's Chic and Youthful Sides

Omotesando-dori is one of those examples of how Tokyo just keeps changing. One hundred years ago, this 0.6-mile-long (one kilometer), tree-lined boulevard functioned as the approach to the then newly constructed Meiji Shrine, which was built to enshrine the souls of the Emperor Meiji and his wife Empress Shoken, but over the years the street has morphed into a focal point for cutting-edge architecture, design and fashion.

Stroll along Omotesando-dori and you pass a succession of plush brand name stores—the likes of Armani, Burberry, Dior, Gucci, and Louis Vuitton—that share the street with some of Tokyo's most interesting architectural sights; none more striking than the Tadao Ando-designed Omotesando Hills, which transformed a large portion of Omotesando-dori when it appeared in the mid-2000s with the Pritzker Prize-winning Ando's characteristic Zen-like simplicity. Hills doesn't go all out on the rough concrete and natural lighting that marks much of the self-taught Ando's work, but his usual stark angles and use of space are all there.

ABOVE Tadao Ando's Omotesando Hills complex is a chic mix of retail, dining, and office space. The inner atrium is a cavernous six-floored space connected by a spiraling ramp—one of Tokyo's most distinctive pieces of architecture by one of the country's most heralded architects. A winner of awards such as the Pritzker, remarkably Ando was self-taught; in his younger days, he worked as a trucker and was a boxer before embarking on his architectural career.

Leave Omotesando-dori behind and the vibe begins to change a little, the backstreets of Omotesando forming a hive of cool cafés and smaller boutiques, places to seek out the work of hip local designers, Scandinavian-influenced interiors and even modern twists on traditional arts and crafts. Haute couture is replaced by urban street fashion, and by the time you get to Harajuku Crossing, youthfulness has taken over. La Foret Harajuku department store here is home to dozens upon dozens of small fashion and accessory stores, while a short walk away is one of the landmark streets of "young Tokyo", Takeshita-dori, a

narrow and crowded side street running toward Harajuku Station where cool and hip are replaced by bright (you might even say gaudy!) teen fashions, cosplay stores, places selling teen-idol merchandise and bucketloads of color. It might not be to everyone's taste, but (especially given Japan's reputation for being rather staid in many respects) you have to tip your hat to the freedom and expressiveness of Tokyo's youth.

On the other side of Harajuku Station comes another drastic change of scenery, with Meiji Shrine and the neighboring

LEFT Omotesando-dori. The vine-covered building was part of the bohemian Dojunkai apartments that were pulled down to make way for Omotesando Hills. This small part was incorporated into the new mall as a nod to the area's past.
ABOVE Shinto wedding processions are a common sight at Meiji Shrine, especially on weekends, when you may see several, one after another.
RIGHT AND TOP RIGHT Inside the grounds of Meiji Shrine.

RIGHT Cosplayers in Yoyogi Park.
OPPOSITE PAGE TOP AND BOTTOM The famous Shibuya Crossing.
OPPOSITE PAGE TOP RIGHT Trendy girls in Shibuya.
OPPOSITE PAGE BOTTOM RIGHT The statue of a dog called Hachiko next to Shibuya Station is a popular meeting point and a favorite tale of loyalty. In the 1930s, the real Hachiko would come to meet his master off the train every day for years, even after his master had died.

TOP Harajuku Station
ABOVE Takeshita-dori is almost always crowded.
RIGHT A crêpe stall on Takeshita-dori. The street has a variety of stalls offering snacks of all varieties.

Yoyogi Park. It's here, in 2020, where the Olympic and Paralympic Games will be centered around a new billion-dollar, oval-shaped lattice-framed stadium designed by Kengo Kuma, while also utilizing some of the legacy of the 1964 Games that includes Kenzo Tange's iconic Yoyogi Gymnasium Stadium and its distinctive suspension roof. Nobody seems sure exactly how much Yoyogi park will change by 2020—hopefully it'll still retain much of its green space and still be one of Tokyo's best spots for people-watching— but thankfully Meiji Shrine will remain just as it was when built in the 1920s to enshrine the Emperor and Empress Meiji; set in seventy acres of forest, it'll still be a remarkably calming city-center retreat where one can spot traditional Shinto wedding processions of a weekend and find some peace and quiet amid its tree-lined walkways.

Forming the third point of a trendsetting triangle with Omotesando and

Harajaku, comes Shibuya. Where Omotesando is cosmopolitan, Shibuya (one station south of Harajuku) is brash. You can stroll along Omotesando-dori, but you fight your way through the oncoming hordes at the landmark Shibuya Crossing. Like Harajuku, Shibuya is younger, too; a hub of teen and twenty-something fashion, where buildings like Shibuya 109 and its hundred or so tiny boutiques spawn the latest trends. And by night, where Omotesando offers chic restaurants and an array of Japanese and international

cuisines, Shibuya is known for its clubs and lively nightlife, which is at its insane best on New Year's Eve (an otherwise calm night in Japan)or when Halloween turns its streets into an all-night fancy dress event.

The Pulsating Heart of Modern Tokyo

If you can navigate Shinjuku Station at rush hour without getting bumped, stuck in a slow-shuffling bottleneck or hopelessly lost, the chances are good you can survive any urban scrum on the planet. More than 3.5 million people pass through the station daily, making it not just one of the busiest in the world and a key commuting hub, but also a place most definitely not for the faint of heart.

The bad news for demophobes is that once you make it out on to the streets of Shinjuku, the crowds tend not to abate. On a work-day morning, the high-rise business district on Shinjuku's west side—the site of skyscraper-capping hotels like the Park Hyatt and the iconic forty-five-story twin towers of the Kenzo Tange-designed Tokyo Metropolitan Government Building—teems with office workers scrambling to make their 9am clock-in. Day and night, the east and south sides can be just as hectic, with people crowding to major department stores like Isetan, Marui, and Takashimaya, a vast range of budget fashion chains, high-end boutiques, sporting-goods stores, and home-electronics stores. And we haven't even mentioned the nightlife yet.

Shinjuku's east-side Kabukicho district is best known as Tokyo's most infamous red-light district, home to all manner of sex clubs (even train-carriage themed clubs where you can pretend to be groping passengers, if that's your scene), host and hostess bars, and yakuza-owned establishments, but is also awash with great izakaya, small music venues, and bars that help give its neon-drenched streets a pulsating energy. Neighboring Kabukicho, the narrow streets and rickety low-rise buildings that make up the Golden-Gai

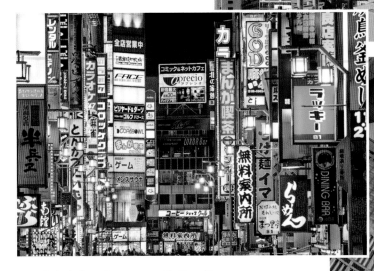

RIGHT The Shinjuku skyline. Mount Fuji hasn't been photoshopped in; you can actually see it on a clear day, especially if you head to the free observation deck atop the Tokyo Metropolitan Government building.

ABOVE The back alleys of Kabukicho in Shinjuku are a seedy playground full of *pachinko* parlors, girlie bars, shops and restaurants of every description.

RIGHT The Kenzo Tange-designed Tokyo Metropolitan Government Building.

LEFT AND BELOW The many side streets of Shinjuku, especially areas like Omoide Yokocho and Hyakunincho, are home to no-frills eateries that are full of character and serve great food.

RIGHT The Robot Restaurant in Shinjuku—complete with bikini-clad dancers, neon, strobes, and futuristic décor—is certainly unlike anything else in the city.

area are even better for a night out, thanks to a collection of tiny bohemian, sometimes friendly, sometimes regulars-only bars that tend to operate on a theme—be that focusing on 60s rock vinyl, acting as a photographer-only hangout or serving their cocktails in syringes and bed pans as part of a hospital thing. And if only drinking doesn't appeal, the "Little Asia" area directly north of Kabukicho (around Okubo and Shin-Okubo stations) is one of Tokyo's great foodie destinations, being not just the focal point for Tokyo's vibrant Korean community (and all its flavors) but also

LEFT Come nightfall, Shinjuku lives up to one Tokyo stereotype that many other areas actually don't—it's bathed in neon and lights.
BELOW The entrance to Kabukicho, Shinjuku's (and Tokyo's most notorious) red-light district. Despite all the sex clubs, gangsters and sleaze, it's quite safe to walk around, and it's also home to hundreds of legitimate bars and restaurants.

ABOVE AND RIGHT Unlike Omotesando and similarly swanky areas, Shinjuku's restaurants have a much more local, Asian feel. There are very few pretenses, just great tastes and a lot of atmosphere.

home to restaurants representing various cuisines of China, Vietnam, Thailand, Myanmar, India, Nepal, and many other parts of Asia.

Given all that, it feels odd that Shinjuku is also the site of one of Tokyo's most tranquil and attractive parks. A ten-minute stroll from Shinjuku Station, the 140 acres (fifty-seven hectares) of Shinjuku Park combine Japanese garden design, English landscaping, and even some formal French styles. More than anything, when spring dapples Japan pink with cherry blossoms, the multiple varieties of *sakura* in Shinjuku Park (plus an entrance fee and no-alcohol policy that protects the peace and quiet) make the park one of Japan's finest places to enjoy the petals in the way nature intended. Year round, it's a lovely calming place to chill out—the yin to the rest of Shinjuku's yang.

Art, Nightlife and "Gaikokujin" World

The good, the bad and on occasion the ugly gather in the Roppongi district—a true mishmash of modern Tokyo. On the one hand, few parts of the city are as cosmopolitan or cultured, yet by night few can be quite as wild. I suppose we should be grateful for progress—because up until the early 2000s, the cultured and cosmopolitan parts were extremely thin on the ground.

When I first came to Tokyo in 1999, Roppongi felt like it was all about nightlife. Thanks in part to its proximity to numerous multinational offices and embassies, the area was (and still is) known for its range of fine international restaurants (fine Japanese ones, too), which rubbed shoulders with a plethora of bars and nightclubs, a mix of meat markets and (then) rare places for an expat to grab a real British, German or American beer away from home. Roppongi wasn't red light per se, but the name certainly conjured up far from salubrious images. Then came a makeover heralded by the opening of Tokyo's first "city within a city" urban redevelopment, the multi-billion dollar Roppongi Hills complex, which opened to incredible hype in 2003 and set the standard for the numerous mega complexes that have since followed in its wake. With a fifty-four-story tower at its center, the multi-building complex mixes office spaces, extremely expensive apartments, one of Tokyo's leading contemporary art galleries (the Mori Art Museum), numerous shops, restaurants, cafés, a multi-screen cinema movie theater, a five-star hotel, an outdoor amphitheater, and even the headquarters of one of Japan's main television networks, Asahi TV.

BELOW The 21_21 Design Sight gallery and workshop at Tokyo Midtown is one of the many contemporary art and design venues in Roppongi. **BELOW LEFT** By day, Roppongi looks much like many other parts of Tokyo. By night, it is very different. **BOTTOM** Louise Bourgeois' *Maman* spider sculpture at Roppongi Hills.

LEFT AND BELOW The Mori Tower of Roppongi Hills. The observation deck tops the fifty-four story main tower at the Roppongi Hills complex, which also houses an art museum and scores of upscale boutiques, cafés and restaurants.
BELOW LEFT By night Roppongi is all about clubs like the 7 Sense (pictured), bars and restaurants.

But one city in a city wasn't enough. A few years later, almost within spitting distance of Roppongi Hills, the Tokyo Midtown complex brought a similarly plush mix of facilities. Not content just to be centered around Tokyo's tallest skyscraper, it also delivered such things as a Ritz-Carlton, the Suntory Museum of Art (and its wonderful collection of traditional Japanese art), and the 21_21 Design Sight gallery and workshop, a collaboration between architect Tadao Ando and fashion designer Issey Miyake that showcases modern Japanese design. Along with Roppongi Hills and venues like the National Art Center, which followed in 2007, Midtown cemented Roppongi's new reputation for being arty, sophisticated, luxurious, fashionable, and numerous other things that (in many places) make it unrecognizable from the Roppongi of the nineties.

Tokyo Tower and Odaiba

The newer southern districts of Tokyo comprise a number of luxurious residential and business neighborhoods where Tokyo's elite live, work and play—Azabu, Hiroo, Daikanyama, Ebisu and Meguro. In the center of it all stands Tower Tower, constructed in 1958 as a broadcasting tower and still one of the city's most iconic sights, while out in Tokyo Bay is the newest district of them all, Odaiba, a manmade island worth a visit for its museums, shops, amusement centers and modern architecture.

LEFT The second tallest structure in Japan, Tokyo Tower at 1,092 feet (333 meters) has amazing views of the city from its observation deck. There's also a small amusement park themed around the Japanese anime *One Piece*.
ABOVE Odaiba's small beach is good for sunbathing, but it's not advisable to wade into the water of Tokyo Bay.
TOP The Rainbow Bridge, which connects Odaiba to mainland Tokyo, and the replica of the Statue of Liberty.

Reached via the now-landmark Rainbow Bridge, which connects the island to mainland Tokyo via road or an unmanned monorail while providing tremendous views back into the city, Odaiba has become a family-friendly mix of malls and other attractions. For starters, it's home to a giant Ferris wheel, cutting-edge amusement centers and amusement parks like Joypolis' mix of high-tech arcade games and virtual reality machines, the slickly designed National Museum of Emerging Science and Innovation (aka Miraikan), a small Legoland Discovery

LEFT The Venus Fort shopping mall.
ABOVE AND MIDDLE RIGHT The headquarters of Fuji TV that also houses the back lot of the *Mezamashi TV* morning show, several shops—and a *One Piece* restaurant.
BELOW RIGHT The kid-friendly Miraikan is arguably the best and coolest science museum in Japan.

Center, and the Oedo-Onsen Monogatari hot-spring theme park, which has a range of indoor and outdoor communal baths, spas, and food stalls and old-fashioned amusements set in Edo-themed interiors.

Mixed in with that, there are architectural oddities like the Kenzo Tange-designed offices of Fuji Television and (I have no idea why it's here) a scaled down replica of the Statue of Liberty. There are commercial sites, too, like Tokyo Big Sight, the city's main convention center, which will be the venue for the wrestling, taekwondo and fencing events at the Tokyo 2020 Olympic Games, while other parts of Odaiba host the kayaking, mountain biking and rowing events.

When you put it all together, you don't find anywhere else in Tokyo with so many entertainment options packed together quite like Odaiba, which goes some way to explaining why Odaiba isn't just a popular destination for families, it's also one of the main date spots for teens.

CHAPTER 2

SIDE TRIPS FROM TOKYO

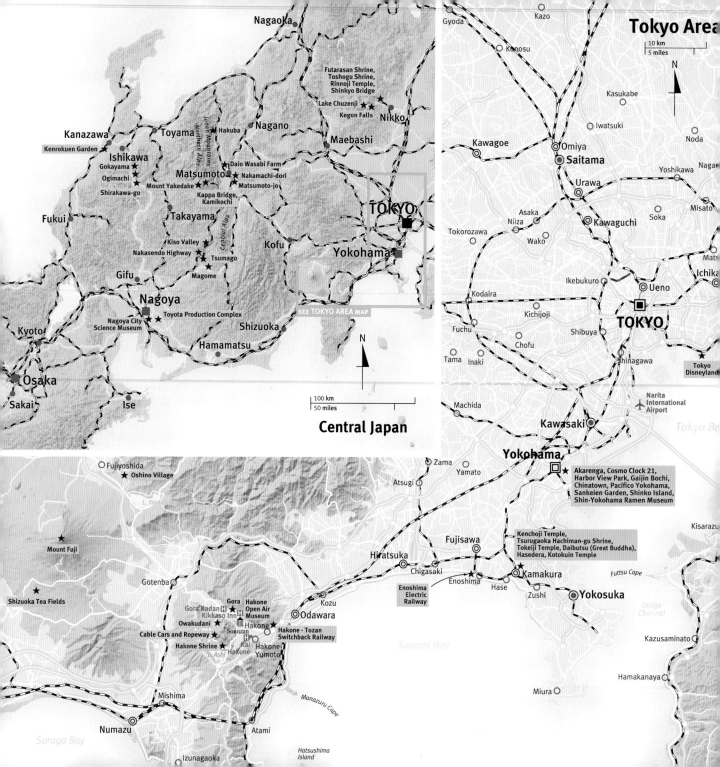

Nagaoka

Futarasan Shrine,
Toshogu Shrine,
Rinnoji Temple,
Shinkyo Bridge

★ Lake Chuzenji ★★
Kegon Falls ★★ Nikko

Joten Mountains
Northern Alps

Kanazawa
★ Hakuba
Toyama Nagano Maebashi

Kenrokuen Garden ★
Ishikawa
Gokayama ★ ★ Daio Wasabi Farm
Ogimachi ★ Matsumoto ★ Nakamachi-dori
Shirakawa-go Mount Yakedake ★ ★ Matsumoto-jo
TOKYO
Kappa Bridge,
Kamikochi

Fukui
Takayama Yokohama
Central Alps

Kiso Valley
Nakasendo Highway ★ ★ Tsumago Kofu
Gifu ★ Magome

Nagoya
Toyota Production Complex
Kyoto Nagoya City Shizuoka
Science Museum
Hamamatsu N

Osaka

Sakai 100 km
Ise 50 miles

Central Japan

SEE TOKYO AREA map

Tokyo Area

Gyoda Kazo
10 km
5 miles
Konosu
N
Kasukabe
Iwatsuki Noda
Kawagoe ○ Omiya
● **Saitama** Yoshikawa Naga
Urawa
Asaka Misato
Niiza Soka
Tokorozawa Wako ◎ **Kawaguchi** Mats
Ikebukuro Ichika
Kodaira ○ **Ueno**
Kichijoji
Fuchu Shibuya ■ **TOKYO**
Chofu
Tama Inaki Shinagawa Tokyo
Disneyland
Machida Narita
International
Kawasaki Airport
Tokyo Bay
Yokohama

Akarenga, Cosmo Clock 21,
Harbor View Park, Gaijin Bochi,
Chinatown, Pacifico Yokohama,
Sankeien Garden, Shinko Island,
Shin-Yokohama Ramen Museum

Fujiyoshida Kisarazu
★ Oshino Village
Zama
L. Yamana Atsugi Yamato

Fujisawa
Mount Fuji ★ Kenchoji Temple,
Tsurugaoka Hachiman-gu Shrine,
Hiratsuka Tokeiji Temple, Daibutsu (Great Buddha),
Chigasaki Hasedera, Kotokuin Temple
Gotenba Kozu ★ Kamakura
Shizuoka Tea Fields ★ Enoshima ★ ★
Gora Kadan H ★ Gora Hase Zushi
Kikkaso Inn Hakone Enoshima Yokosuka
Owakudani ★ Open Air Electric Uraga
Cable Cars and Ropeway ★ Hakone Museum Railway Channel
Sounzan Kai Hakone - Tozan Kazusaminato
Hakone Shrine ★ Hakone Switchback Railway
L. Ashi Hakone Yumoto Odawara Sagami Bay
Hamakanaya

Mishima Miura
Manazuru Cape
Numazu Atami
Izunagaoka Suraga Bay Hatsushima
Island

Kashimayari, Nagano

Great Buddha, Kamakura

Akechidaira Ropeway, Nikko

Mount Fuji

UNMISSABLE SIDETRIPS FROM TOKYO

Just beyond Tokyo, the modern is punctuated by fine examples of ancient and natural Japan. Heading west comes Kamakura, the thirteenth-century political and spiritual capital, with its collection of shrines, temples and famed giant Buddha, while to the north in Nikko the Toshogu Shrine of first Edo shogun, Tokugawa Ieyasu, is one of Japan's most decadently decorated sites. Then there is Yokohama, bordering Tokyo to the south west, the fishing village that rapidly became a major, thriving port when Japan opened its borders in the Meiji era. Beyond that comes somewhere that cannot be overlooked—literally on clear days from central Tokyo—the iconic Mount Fuji, then go a little further west and you have the magnificent Japan Alps, to the north of which lies historic Kanazawa, which like many of the Alps' villages seems in places to have been frozen in time.

Yabusame Festival, Kamakura

Matsumoto Castle

Toshogu Shrine, Nikko

Yokohama

Kanto's Historic Port City

Yokohama's history is brief, but its rise spectacular. Before Japan ended its Edo-era *sakoku* policy of (near) isolation, the city (of now 3.5 million people) was one of many small fishing villages barely marking a dot on the coastline. After the U.S. naval ships led by Commodore Matthew Perry appeared in the bay in 1853 and initiated a treaty that would eventually open up Japan, Yokohama boomed.

Despite having been sheltered from the outside for more than two hundred years, Japan's and especially Yokohama's internationalization was incredibly swift. It was less than ten years after Perry arrived in what the Japanese disparagingly called his "Black Ships" that Yokohama's lively *chukagai* (Chinatown) was established. The area has become not just the center of a vibrant Chinese community but also one of Yokohama's main attractions, pulling in some eighteen million visitors annually with the area's two hundred or so restaurants and three hundred specialty shops.

RIGHT Yokohama's harbor-front skyline. The Landmark Tower dominates on the left, then moving right you see the old Akarenga warehouses. On the far right, the slightly curved building is part of Pacifico Yokohama, Japan's largest convention complex.

ABOVE AND LEFT Yokohama's Chinatown has been thriving since shortly after Japan reopened itself to the rest of the world in the 1850s, and is one of the main attractions in the area for local tourists. Mostly that's because of its range of Chinese cuisine, but also because it oozes a very un-Japanese and vibrant vibe.

Other areas from Yokohama's early post-*sakoku* development are less busy. One popular with Japanese tourists is the Gaijin Bochi (Foreigner's Cemetery), a Western-style graveyard perched on a hill that overlooks the bay. Some of the three thousand graves here have fascinating stories to tell about the risks and adventures the early outsiders faced in the newly opened Japan—like British merchant Charles Richardson, whose murder by men loyal to Lord Satsuma in 1862 was the catalyst for the Anglo-Satsuma War of 1863.

Down on the waterfront you get an interesting mix of old and new. In Harbor View Park, which was the site of a British garrison until 1870 (there to protect traders and settlers), are a handful of Western-

RIGHT In the shadow of the Landmark Tower, the Nippon Maru is a former training ship built in 1930. By the time she was retired in 1984, she'd clocked up almost 1,080 nautical miles (two million kilometers) at sea, in the process having helped trained twelve thousand cadets. In her retirement, she is absolutely beautiful to explore—a lovely remnant of Yokohama's earlier days.

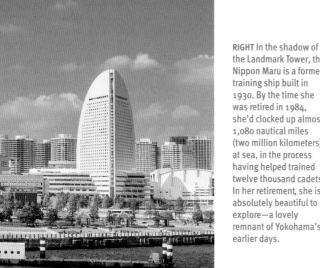

BELOW Sankeien Garden in Yokohama's Naka Ward, built by silk trader Tomitaro Hara. Ten of the structures in this Japanese-style garden have been classified as Important Cultural Property.

LEFT Yokohama isn't famous for any particular ramen style of its own; instead it has the Shin-Yokohama Ramen Museum, which brings together famous ramen shops (and varieties) from around Japan. If you are wondering about the unusual design, it is meant to represent how Japan would have looked in 1958, when cup ramen was invented.

influenced buildings dating to the early Meiji period. Then there is the man-made Shinko Island, which has more historic structures in the form of the Akarenga: two long, low red brick warehouses built in 1911 that now form a waterfront entertainment, shopping and dining complex. And to remind anyone that might have forgotten that Yokohama is now a modern city, the Akarenga shares a skyline with the 353-foot-high (107.5 meter) Cosmo Clock 21 Ferris wheel (for a while the world's largest) and a towering high rise backdrop that reflects on to the bay.

A Visit to Japan's Ancient Seaside Capital

As day trips from Tokyo go, it's hard to beat Kamakura, the town that from 1192–1333 was the cultural, political and spiritual center of Japan. Known as the Kamakura era, that period came about after the Genpei War of 1180–85, which saw the Minamoto clan defeat the Taira clan and under leader Yoritomo Minamoto soon after begin 140 years of rule that have left Kamakura awash with magnificent remnants from its golden age.

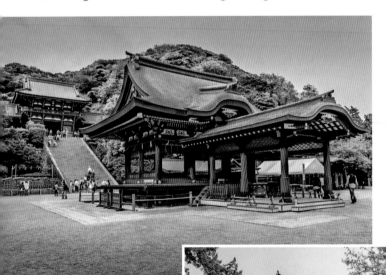

ABOVE The grounds of Tsurugaoka Hachimangu, which was enlarged and moved to its current site in 1180 by Yoritomo Minamoto.
RIGHT Kenchoji Temple was commissioned by Emperor Go-Fukakusa and was completed in 1253.
TOP Kamakura looks out to Sagami Bay, with Mount Fuji looming large to the west.

That heritage includes some of the Kanto region's finest historic structures. Representing Shintoism, Japan's indigenous religion, is the Tsurugaoka Hachimangu Shrine, which in September offers a glimpse back at the Kamakura era when it hosts the annual Reitaisai Festival—known for its procession in period costumes and performance of *yabusame* horseback archery. Any time of year, however, a visit is worthwhile just to check out the shrine itself, in particular the towering vermilion lacquered *torii* gateway at its entrance after which follows a straight road leading to steps up to the main hall perched high up among woods. A closer inspection of the grounds will also bring you to the shrine's Heike and Gempei ponds, which paint a grim picture of life in feudal Japan; supposedly, the two ponds were designed by the wife of Yoritomo Minamoto, with

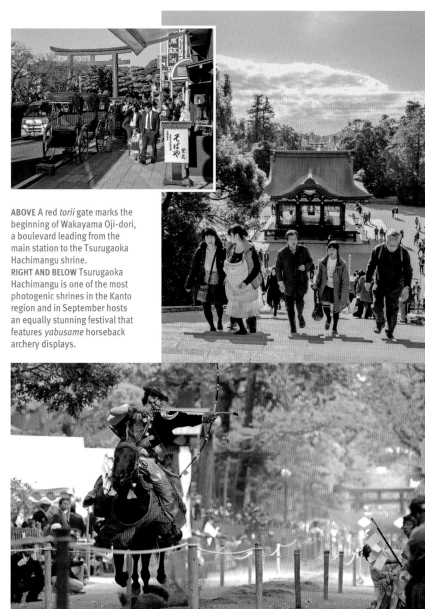

ABOVE A red *torii* gate marks the beginning of Wakayama Oji-dori, a boulevard leading from the main station to the Tsurugaoka Hachimangu shrine.
RIGHT AND BELOW Tsurugaoka Hachimangu is one of the most photogenic shrines in the Kanto region and in September hosts an equally stunning festival that features *yabusame* horseback archery displays.

the three islands in Gempei being based on the Chinese character for victory to symbolize the Minamoto clan's dominance over the Taira clan, and the four islands in Heike representing the death of the Minamoto's enemies (phonetically "four" sounds like "death" in Japanese).

Buddhism has left an even greater mark on modern-day Kamakura. To reel off just a couple of the ancient temples worth visiting in the city, you could start with Kenchoji, founded in 1253 and not only the head temple of the Rinzai sect of Buddhism but also Japan's oldest Zen training monastery, which at its peak is said to have had forty-nine sub-temples. Then there is thirteenth-century Tokeiji, a former nunnery that is arguably one of the best places in Kamakura to see how entwined spiritualism and tradition have become with an appreciation of nature, in

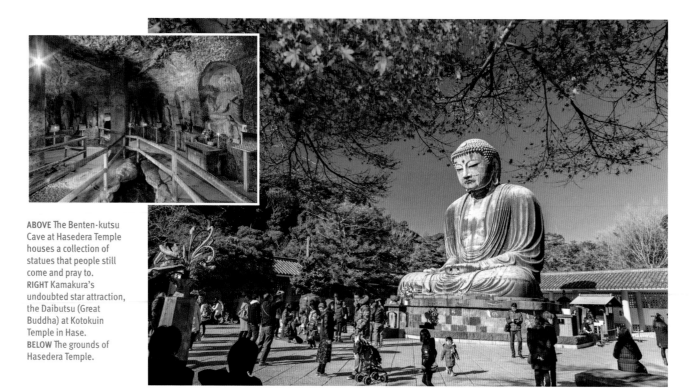

ABOVE The Benten-kutsu Cave at Hasedera Temple houses a collection of statues that people still come and pray to.
RIGHT Kamakura's undoubted star attraction, the Daibutsu (Great Buddha) at Kotokuin Temple in Hase.
BELOW The grounds of Hasedera Temple.

Tokeiji's case with an ever-changing backdrop of flora and fauna that includes apricot blossoms in February, magnolias in March and irises in June.

Nothing, however, has the allure of Kamakura's star attraction, found a few stations away on the quaint Enoshima Electric Railway (nicknamed Enoden) at Kotokuin Temple in Hase—the Daibutsu (Great Statue of Buddha). Now 750 years old, the 44-foot-tall (13-meter) Buddha, eyes closed and cross-legged in meditation, has taken a bit of a battering, losing the hall that once sheltered him from a tsunami in

RIGHT Just offshore from the nearest sandy beaches to Tokyo and Yokohama, the island of Enoshima is a mere two-and-a-half miles (four kilometers) in circumference, connected to the mainland by a narrow isthmus.

1495 and, some argue, losing the gilding he may have been born with.

Apart from the Daibutsu, Hase is also home to a pleasant stretch of beach—Yuigahama—near which a number of restaurants serve a Kamakura-area signature dish called *shirasu-don*, rice topped with heaps of tiny whitebait. There's another temple worth visiting here, too, Hasedera, known for a 30-foot-high (nine-meter) gilded statue of Kannon carved from a single piece of camphor wood in Nara sometime in the eighth century, plus a collection of small *Jizo* (guardian deity of children) statues. Mixed in with the Daibutsu and all the sights of Kamakura proper, it's no wonder this jaunt west is such a popular day trip with Tokyoites.

RIGHT The beaches around Kamakura attract sunbathers and (although not great for surfing) casual water sports fans. Near the beaches, you'll find quite a few pleasant cafés and restaurants, some of the latter serving a Kamakura specialty called *shirasu-don*—a bowl of rice topped with piles of extremely young (and tiny) whitebait.

ABOVE Not the famous bamboo grove in Kyoto, but Kamakura's less heralded version, which is found at Hokokuji Temple.
LEFT *Nagomi Jizo* smiling-monk statues, said to promote good relationships.

ABOVE The Enoden Line connecting Kamakura with Hase and Enoshima is a quaint throwback. On a weekday, you can enjoy glimpses of local neighborhoods and coastal views from the two-car train. On weekends, it's good practice for a rugby scrum.

Soothing Hot Springs and Iconic Views of Japan's Most Sacred Mountain

No other natural site has had anywhere near the kind of influence on Japan as Mount Fuji, affectionately called Fuji-san. With almost perfect symmetry and dominating the skyline far and wide from her position straddling the prefectures of Shizuoka and Yamanashi, Japan's tallest peak has had everyone from artists to entire religions under her spell over the centuries.

The most iconic images of Mount Fuji—a common sight on postcards and tourist goods from tee shirts to mouse mats—are the *ukiyo-e* (woodblock prints) of Japan's most revered printmaker, Katsuhika Hokusai (1760–1849), who dedicated much of his working life to capturing Fuji-san. His *Great Wave Off Kanagawa,* from the series *Thirty-six Views of Mount Fuji,* is one of the most famous images not just of Fuji, but of Japan itself, with a snow-capped Fuji depicted in the distance as a menacing wave readies to break in the foreground.

The 12,388-foot (3,776-meter) dormant volcano is also a sacred site in both indigenous Shintoism and imported Buddhism; in the former as the home of a fire goddess (amongst other spirits) and in the latter the home of Dainichi Nyorai, the Buddha of All-Illuminating Wisdom. It was supposedly because of the fire goddess's jealousy of other women (and perhaps a

fear that her wrath would lead to an eruption of Fuji) that women were prohibited from climbing Fuji-san until 1868. Japan might still not have the most stellar reputation when it comes to such things as gender equality in the workplace, but at least at Fuji all is now straight: in the July–August climbing season, men, women, Japanese, non-Japanese, even kids (some 250,000 people in all) make a six- to eight-hour trek in an attempt to watch the sun rise from atop the mountain.

You can see Fuji-san from all sorts of places, even from many parts of central Tokyo when the weather cooperates, but for Tokyoites the most popular way to get up close to the mountain is with an overnight

LEFT It's not hard to see why Fuji has captivated so many artists over the centuries. By day or night, whichever season, and from each direction, the region's dominant peak frequently leaves people lost for words.

RIGHT, MIDDLE RIGHT AND BOTTOM RIGHT It's not the easiest of climbs if you aren't used to hiking, but time the ascent just right and you will be rewarded with a magical sunrise from the top of Fuji.

OPPOSITE PAGE BOTTOM Historic thatched buildings at Oshino (known for its eight clear-water ponds) near Mount Fuji.

BELOW Fuji-san seen from the tea fields of Shizuoka Prefecture, which produces some of Japan's finest green tea.

ABOVE For many this is the classic Hakone image, and it is at its very best in the autumn when Fuji is snow-capped and the dense woods around Lake Ashi take on seasonal rusts and yellows.

LEFT The galleon-like design of the boat is questionable, but a trip out on the lake is nevertheless a lot of fun.

FAR LEFT AND BELOW A man stops to pray at Hakone Shrine, which also offers idyllic views of Lake Ashi. A path from the main building leads to the monument that celebrates the post-World War II peace treaty.

LEFT The ropeways and cable cars used to navigate much of the classic Hakone sightseeing route provide magnificent mountain views.

trip to the natural scenery, ryokan (traditional inns) and *onsen (*hot spring baths) of the Hakone area, just sixty-two miles (100 kilometers) west of central Tokyo. The traditional way to explore Hakone is well worn, but still very worthwhile, starting at Hakone-Yumoto with the two-carriage Hakone-Tozan switchback railway on a slow, zigzagging route ending at the village of Gora (perhaps with a stop at the Hakone Open-Air Museum on the way), where the next leg is a funicular train up to the 2,625-foot (800-meter) Sounzan (Mount Soun). After that, tourists tend to transfer to a cable car that runs over the volcanic valley of Owakudani (literally, "Great Boiling Valley"), full of bubbling hot-spring pools and steaming sulfur vents, before the cable heads down from the mountains to Lake Ashi. To cap it all, Lake Ashi provides the classic view of Hakone—Fuji (often capped with snow) in the background behind the lake's blue waters and lush rim, which is accented by the vermilion gateway of Hakone Shrine.

ABOVE, TOP AND LEFT The geothermal activity in the area provides natural hot-spring waters that are employed in simple (but very relaxing) public footbaths and the *onsen* baths one finds at ryokan (traditional inns). For a special weekend away, Hakone has some top ryokan—Gora Kadan, Kikasso and Kai Hakone to name just a few. Additionally, try the blackened eggs cooked by the piping hot steam from the pools and vents of Owakudani.

A Memorial to Japan's First Shogun

Given that the Toshogu Shrine in Nikko was built to enshrine one of Japan's greatest historical figures, Tokugawa Ieyasu, the man who united Japan and became the first shogun of the 265-year Edo era, it probably shouldn't be a surprise that it's one of the country's most lavishly built sites. Located 75 miles (120 kilometers) north of Tokyo in largely rural Tochigi Prefecture, the peaceful natural setting of Ieyasu's resting place couldn't be more of a contrast to the buildings that hold his spirit.

ABOVE The original three monkeys come from Tendai Buddhism—hear no evil, speak no evil, see no evil.
BELOW LEFT AND RIGHT The Toshogu complex is wonderfully over the top in color. One of the most decadently built shrines in Japan, it's a worthy World Heritage Site and a striking backdrop for a range of annual events and festivals.

Just look at the shrine's Yomeimon (Sun Blaze Gate), a 36-foot (11-meter) high roofed gateway that's a vivid mix of black, gold, red and green adorned with more than five hundred carvings of birds, dancing maidens, dragons and flowers, or study the hundreds of similar decorations on the shrine's deep-red five-story pagoda, and when you add it all up it's easy to see why Toshogu's two-year construction involved fifteen thousand craftsmen and a staggering 2.5 million sheets of gold leaf. There are other Toshogu shrines in Japan, but none of them come close to the decadence of Nikko.

Beside the almost garish, however, there's also a lot of subtlety. One of the most famous points of interest, even though it's so small that many people miss it, is a carving of the Three Wise Monkeys, which represents the three main principles of Tendai Buddhism—the concept of "Hear no evil, speak no evil, see no evil". Equally easy to miss is the tiny carving of a sleeping cat (the *nemuri neko*), which supposedly dates back to the sixteenth century and a famous Edo-era sculptor called Hidari Jingoro; although one oddity here is that, rather like certain Shakespeare theories, some people doubt Jingoro ever existed at all.

And, of course, Toshogu isn't all there is to Nikko. Within minutes of Toshogu are the Tendai sect's Rinnoji Temple complex, whose main hall is home to three giant gilded Buddha and Kannon statues,

LEFT The Shinkyo Bridge. After a long restoration in the 2000s, the vermilion bridge once used by shoguns is once again radiant. When the water is flowing and frothy, and autumn is in full color, it has to be the defining Nikko image.

ABOVE A statue of the first Edo shogun, Tokugawa Ieyasu, for whom the Toshogu complex was built. LEFT The Taiyuin Mausoleum (for Tokugawa Iemitsu, Ieyasu's grandson) at Rinnoji Temple.

and—rounding out the three sites that make up Nikko's World Heritage listing— the more understated Futarasan Shrine. Also nearby is the Shinkyo Bridge, a small vermilion-colored footbridge originally used by feudal lords and their entourages to cross the Daiya River on route to Toshogu—nowadays it's one of Nikko's most photographed views. Much further away, on a winding forty-minute bus trip, is the stunning nature of the Kegon Falls and Lake Chuzenji, both of which are especially attractive when autumnal colors repaint the wooded mountains that enshroud the lake. The falls cascade some 328 feet (100 meters), and the views from near the bottom, which can be reached by elevator, are one reason they are vaunted as one of Japan's most attractive three waterfalls (Japan loves its top-three rankings!). Just watch out for the monkeys at the lake; as the unintentionally comical warning posters around Chuzenji will tell you, there are lots of simian pickpockets about who love to grab snacks, shopping and anything else they can get their hairy little hands on.

RIGHT Kegon Falls, with Lake Chuzenji in the background. Many day trippers don't get up here, but with an early start from Tokyo (or better, a night at a traditional inn in Nikko), a trip to Chuzenji adds another dimension to Nikko with a glimpse at the kind of natural beauty much of rural Japan is blessed with.

Stunning Mountain Scenery and Enduring Cultural Traditions

Just over 93 miles (150 kilometers) northwest of Tokyo, in the majestic Northern Alps of Nagano Prefecture, the city of Matsumoto is the gateway to some of Japan's most stunning scenery and its finest hiking routes. The city itself initially flourished as a castle town after the five-tiered, six-story castle was constructed into its current form here in the 1590s, making it the oldest original castle remaining in Japan. It's certainly a striking sight, with the main 98-foot-high (30-meter) donjon and other buildings forming a 656-yard (600-meter) square that to feudal forces must have appeared impenetrable. And away from the castle you can still see traces of the wealth that the castle brought to the town, too, especially in the form of the white-walled *kura-zukuri* warehouses on the old Nakamachi-dori road.

LEFT Children get dressed up for Shichi-Go-San in Matsumoto. This festival is a nationwide rite of passage for three and seven-year-old girls and three and five-year-old boys.
FAR LEFT Majestic Matsumoto Castle.

For hikers, just to the west of Matsumoto is Kamikochi. 4,593 feet (1,500 meters) above sea level, this scenic basin is surrounded by prime hiking areas—some extremely challenging, with fatalities an annual occurrence—including Mount Yakedake, the Jonen Mountains, and the Hotaka Mountain Range. While to the south of Matsumoto, in the Central Alps, there're some easier walking opportunities—rambles into the past—on the old Nakasendo highway in the Kiso Valley. The Kisoji road, the 43-mile (70-kilometer) section of the Nakasendo route that connected Kyoto and Edo (now Tokyo) during the Edo era, leads from

Nagano into Gifu Prefecture and is dotted with former staging-post towns, including the neighboring Magome and Tsumago, where the preserved wooden buildings and stone pathways combine with mountain scenery to make it feel like you are somehow stepping back in time.

There's more history to discover deeper into Gifu, too. The city of Takayama, like the Kisoji road, is steeped in tradition; known for its fine sake, traditional crafts, and preserved neighborhoods. And from Takayama, it's easy to reach one of the jewels in Japan's tourism crown—the villages of the Shirakawa-go and Gokayama regions. Ogimachi, the most famous of the

ABOVE Kamikochi is the starting point for many of Japan's best hikes. But even if you don't want to take on the challenging climbs and prefer a more leisurely visit, the area's stunning beauty is worth the trip.
RIGHT The Kappa Bridge is famous in Kamikochi. *Kappa* are mythical creatures living in water who are said to lure away children. If you were to see one (legend says), you should bow. The *kappa*'s weakness is politeness. It'll bow back, making it lose the water in the bowl on its head that gives it its strength.
BELOW Travelers rowing down the river for a scenic tour of the Daio Wasabi Farm in Azumino City in Matsumoto.

ABOVE Winter sports were big in this part of Japan long before Nagano hosted the 1998 Winter Olympics, but since then ski villages like Hakuba have become popular with overseas travelers, too. The quality of the skiing and snowboarding here is excellent and on the whole the resorts are well geared to serving non-Japanese speakers.
BELOW The small town of Magome, a historic post town on the old Nakasendo trail between Kyoto and Edo, via the mountainous inland route.

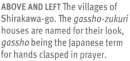

ABOVE AND LEFT The villages of Shirakawa-go. The *gassho-zukuri* houses are named for their look, *gassho* being the Japanese term for hands clasped in prayer.

ABOVE Fresh wasabi. Trying it freshly grated as opposed to from a tube (although that's the norm for most Japanese) is an entirely different experience. (What is sold as "wasabi" in Western countries is often just green-colored mustard; fresh wasabi has a totally different taste.)
RIGHT AND FAR RIGHT This part of Japan has a rich heritage of arts and crafts, some of which you can try for yourself through special workshops.

villages, is like something from a fairytale, its steeply thatched *gassho-zukuri* farmhouses set against lush green rice paddies in summer and then thick in snow in winter.

Heading north from Gifu, into Ishikawa Prefecture, the coastal city of Kanazawa—now reachable from Tokyo by bullet train—is another traditional highlight. As well as a center for centuries-old crafts such as *Kaga-yuzen* dyed silk, vivid *kutaniyaki* pottery, and *Kanazawa-haku* gold-leaf craftworking, Kanazawa is home to several historic districts, including the Teramachi area and its seventy or so small temples. Nothing, however, is as famous here as Kenrokuen Garden— ranked along with Kairakuen Garden in Mito and the Korakuen Garden in Okayama as one of the country's top three gardens. Started in the 1670s, it supposedly took 170 years to finish the 26 acre (105,000-square-meter) garden, which is known for its use of *yukitsuri* ropes over the trees to protect them from heavy snowfall.

LEFT, BELOW AND MIDDLE RIGHT Ranked as one of Japan's three finest traditional gardens, Kenrokuen in Kanazawa is one of the region's not-to-be-missed sites. **BOTTOM LEFT AND RIGHT** Kanazawa has plenty to see, ranging from its historic gardens and bustling fish market to the stunning architecture of Kanazawa Station. And now that the bullet train connects Tokyo to Kanazawa, it's an easy journey; there are no excuses not to go see it all.

CHAPTER 3
KYOTO AND THE KANSAI REGION

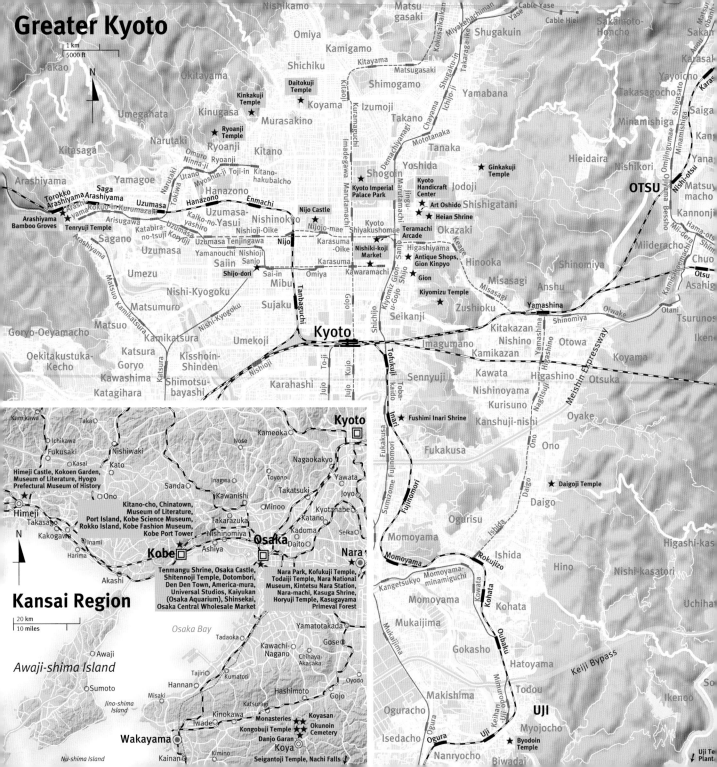

Ryoanji Temple

Fushimi Inari Shrine

Kaiseki cuisine

Maiko

INTRODUCING KYOTO AND KANSAI

No part of Japan has the diversity of attractions found in the Kansai region. Comprising the prefectures of Hyogo, Kyoto, Mie, Nara, Osaka, Shiga, and Wakayama, the region incorporates bits of everything that makes Japan special, from the historic attractions, traditional cuisines and World Heritage Sites of Kyoto and Nara to the dynamic, commercial city of Osaka and the spiritual surrounds of Mount Koya.

Tea Ceremony

Dotonbori Hotel, Osaka

Train Sushi Bar

Kinkakuji Temple

Japan's Ancient Cultural Heartland

As Japan's capital from 794 to 1868, albeit with a hiatus during the Kamakura era from 1192 to 1333, Kyoto was at the heart of Japan's cultural, spiritual and political growth for almost a thousand years. Shintoism and Buddhism flourished here, leaving behind a legacy of shrines, gardens and temples that today make up the majority of the city's historic attractions. Cultural traditions like the tea ceremony, kimono textile weaving and ikebana flower arranging have been honed and perfected here. Culinary traditions, too. Although Kyoto today is a modern, thriving city with a population of 1.5 million, which ranks it as Japan's eighth most populous city, the new certainly hasn't eclipsed the best of the old. North, south, east or west—whichever part of Kyoto you visit, the past is never far away.

BELOW Nobody knows for sure who designed the fifteenth-century raked sand garden at Ryoanji Temple or what it symbolizes— some say the rocks are a map to Chinese temples, others believe they represent a tiger carrying a cub across a stream—but it's said if you can see all fourteen rocks from a single vantage point (without the aid of a drone or selfie stick!), you have reached enlightenment.

LEFT One of the seventeen sites in Kyoto given joint World Heritage status in 1994, Kinkakuji (aka the Golden Pavilion) was originally built in the late 1300s as a villa for the shogun Ashikaga Yoshimitsu and then transformed into a Zen temple upon his death. The current version, though, is surprisingly new—it was rebuilt in the 1950s after a crazed monk burnt it down.

L ook to the northwest and you see a contrasting pair of temples that are among Japan's most iconic sights—Ryoanji and its dry-landscape garden, which features a cryptic arrangement of rocks on raked sand, and the gilded Kinkakuji, which casts a golden reflection onto the waters before it. Both temples have been designated as UNESCO World Heritage Sites, as have almost a dozen other locations around Kyoto, including Kinkakuji's unadorned cousin Ginkakuji (lit., silver pavilion) in the northeast of the city. Oddly, where Kinkakuji lives up to its name, Ginkakuji doesn't have an ounce of silver on it (it's said the people behind it ran out of money and couldn't afford the planned silver), but the understated wooden structure is a perfect fit for its natural surrounds.

In the central part of Kyoto, though built-up like other Japanese cities, a series of attractions punctuates the concrete city spaces. The Gion district is arguably the most photographed of Kyoto's sights because of its old wooden buildings and

RIGHT Although Kyoto is largely a very modern city, traditional ceremonies and festivals are still a regular sight.
BELOW Ginkakuji Temple in northeastern Kyoto was built by the grandson of the shogun who built the gilded Kinkakuji Temple, and like Kinkakuji it switched from villa to Zen temple upon the shogun's death.

the kimono-clad geisha who flit between appointments in Gion's exclusive teahouses. Add to that historic locations like Nijo Castle, the Heian Shrine and Kyoto Imperial Palace Park, plus shopping and foodie destinations that we will come to in a few minutes.

Head eastward from the Gion area and you get more World Heritage Sites with Kiyomizu Temple, where the distinctive veranda, supported on pillars and jutting out from a lush hillside, is an iconic Kyoto landmark, providing a spectacular view of the city. Go on a jaunt to western Kyoto and you get to the Arashiyama area and its eerie bamboo groves. Take a day trip south and there's the green tea and sake of Uji

town (also home to Byodoin, the temple on the back of the ten-yen coin) as well as the photogenic *torii* gateways that cover the sprawling grounds of Fushimi Inari Shrine. Whichever part of Kyoto you look at, there's so much history to see that you will never run out of things to do in this area.

ABOVE Trainee geisha (or *geiko* to use the Kyoto term) are referred to as *maiko*.
LEFT Restaurant lanterns (this one says "tempura") illuminate many of Kyoto's streets at night, including this one at Karasuma.
TOP LEFT The Karamon Gate to Nijo Castle.
TOP RIGHT Kyoto is a great city to walk or cycle around, and it has an excellent subway and bus network, but if you have no hang-ups about looking touristy, a rickshaw ride can be fun too.

LEFT A *maiko* (trainee geisha). *Maiko* have more elaborate hair accessories than geisha and also wear high wooden sandals, not flat *zori* or *geta* sandals.

RIGHT The streets leading to and from Kiyomizu Temple are home to old wooden buildings that house traditional craft and souvenir stores, cafés and restaurants.

BELOW Kiyomizu Temple's distinctive veranda. A Japanese expression similar to "take the plunge" comes from here, because until the practice was banned in the late Edo era, it was said if you jumped from the 43-foot (13-meter) platform and survived, your wishes would be granted.

ABOVE Byodoin (Byodo means "symmetry" in Japanese) in Uji is the temple on the back of the ¥10 coin. Originally built in 1053, the main hall is also referred to as the Phoenix Hall as it is said to resemble a phoenix spreading its wings. Inside, it holds priceless treasures dating to the Heian era (794–1185).

Beyond looking at the past, a stay in Kyoto also means the opportunity to get hands-on with traditional Japanese culture like nowhere else; to immerse yourself in old Japan. You can try Zen meditation, the tea ceremony, cooking classes, and workshops for dozens of traditions—things like pottery and tie-dying. Browsing Kyoto's stores is another great way to get up close to its traditional arts and crafts. The Kyoto Handicraft Center, as just one example, is home to such things as woodblock prints, Nambu ironware, lacquerware, ceramics, kimono and *yukata* robes, and many other arts, crafts and souvenirs. Explore the dozens of antique shops just north of Gion on Furumonzen and Shinmonzen streets and you can find everything from furniture to calligraphy items and armor. Wander the covered Teramachi arcade, which runs northward from the central street called Shijo-dori, and there are even more traditional stores.

And, of course, when in Kyoto you can eat some of Japan's finest foods. Running west along a narrow, covered street from Teramachi's

ABOVE The oft-photographed vermilion *torii* gates at Fushimi Inari Shrine. Avoid the crowds by going early. LEFT Arashiyama in western Kyoto is a popular half-day outing. In spring, you can picnic under cherry blossoms by the southern end of the river running through the area, while in fall boat trips upstream take in stunning gorges and autumnal colors. And any time of year, don't miss the area's bamboo grove (see the image on page 72–73).

LEFT AND RIGHT (all) Some of the many traditional arts and crafts which have been perfected over centuries in Kyoto. The shop on the left, Art Oshido, is a leading dealer of fine Japanese antique pieces, located with a group of other antique stores to the north of Gion.

BELOW The main street in Uji is full of places to buy and sample high-grade green teas grown from the surrounding tea fields, the second-largest production area in Japan.

southern end, the historic Nishiki Market is a foodie's dream, with upward of a hundred shops between them offering an exploration of Kyoto cuisine. There are dried fish specialists, pickle stores, tofu shops, sweet parlors, and many others, not to mention places selling high-end knives and all sorts of cooking utensils. Stay at one of Kyoto's many fine ryokan (traditional inns) and as well as experiencing a night on a futon in a tatami-mat room defined by touches like paper screen doors, you will get to indulge in a multi-course *Kyo-ryori* dinner—a succession of small, beautifully

RIGHT Many restaurant interiors can be very traditional, especially at places serving classic food like *Kyo-ryori*, or *shojin ryori* (Buddhist vegetarian cuisine), with low tables on tatami matting and maybe even views onto landscaped gardens.

ABOVE When in Kyoto, instead of drinking coffee, try some of the many types of green and other local tea.
RIGHT Nishiki Market. As well as produce like pickles, tofu, teas, dried fish, and so on, you can pick up some great snacks here—maybe some skewered sparrow meat if you are feeling brave, or some conventional *yakitori*, fresh sea urchin in its shell, or grilled scallops.

ABOVE *Machiya* rental townhouses are an atmospheric and private alternative to staying at a ryokan or hotel. This one, Gion Kinpyo, was once a sake brewery.

TOP RIGHT An *irori* open hearth. You might eat around one of these at some of the more rustic ryokan.

LEFT Dinner at a ryokan is a multi-course affair featuring a succession of beautifully presented dishes made with an emphasis on in-season and local produce.

RIGHT Kyoto's ryokan don't tend to have the large indoor and outdoor communal hot-spring baths you find in places like Hakone or Atami, but they often have gently scented cedar or cypress baths with piping hot water that soothes away any aches, pains and stress.

presented dishes using local specialties and seasonal produce. Beyond the confines of a ryokan, there are numerous *Kyo-ryori* restaurants around Kyoto (just be prepared to drop a lot of money; or go for the much cheaper lunch sampler), and places to try equally refined vegetarian *shojin ryori*, tempura, sushi, and more. To round off a full Kyoto experience, you need to try it at least once.

Where Cultural Japan Emerged

Often referred to as the birthplace of Japanese civilization, Nara is the only place in Japan that comes close to topping Kyoto for tradition. In and leading up to the city's tenure as Japan's capital from 710 to 794, it was in Nara where the social structures, religious traditions and many other cultural aspects of traditional Japan really took shape. Nara has of course since developed into a modern city with a population pushing 400,000, although what makes it still so special is that unlike Kyoto, which followed Nara as capital, many of the historic attractions stand together, removed from the city's modern quarters, giving Nara an older and calmer vibe that makes a day there well worth the simple 25-mile (40-kilometer) trip from Kyoto.

For many visitors Nara begins with Nara Park, a short walk from Kintetsu Nara Station where many arrive from Kyoto, and it takes only seconds here before they start meeting Nara's most famous residents, the semi-tame deer that call Nara Park home and in cartoon form adorn all sorts of products (from cookies to t-shirts) in Nara's souvenir stores. The park can get crowded in parts with tourists, yet much of it is tranquil and pastoral, a remarkable city-center swathe of greenery in and around which are some of Nara's main historic attractions.

The first of these to greet visitors is the seventh-century Kofukuji Temple on Nara Park's western side, known for its six hundred-year-old five-story pagoda and a priceless collection of Buddhist artifacts that includes one of Japan's most famous sculptures in the form of an eighth-century standing representation of the three-headed, six-armed Ashura. In the heart of the park, there's more history on display at Nara National Museum, a Western-style stone building built in the Meiji era that houses a broad collection of Japanese and

BELOW The deer living in Nara Park have become the symbol of the city. Semi tame, you can feed them *shika sembei* (deer crackers) sold by vendors all around the park, although as the comical manga-like warning posters point out, beware—the *shika* sometimes charge, bite and headbutt the hand that feeds them!

RIGHT AND TOP Nara Park is a lovely space to relax in, with several teahouses and rest areas serving refreshments like green tea and traditional sweets.
TOP RIGHT Part of the Todaiji Temple complex.
MIDDLE RIGHT The deer get everywhere, even to World Heritage Sites like the Nandaimon Gate to Todaiji Temple.

RIGHT Staff at Kofukuji Temple writing out devotional calligraphy sheets that are sold to visitors.

other Asian art and artifacts, but that's really just a teaser for what's to come at the north and east ends.

Stroll to Nara Park's eastern quadrant and you get Kasuga Shrine, originally built in 786 and known for the photogenic rows of stone lanterns that line the approach to the main shrine building, where several thousand equally photogenic bronze lanterns give Kasuga its distinctive look. Head north, passing touristy souvenir stores and hordes of deer begging for snacks, and you get Nara's star attraction, Todaiji Shrine. Built over fifteen years during the first half of the 700s by the Emperor Shomu, the complex is famously home to one of the world's largest wooden buildings, the 187-foot-long (57-meter) and 164-foot-wide (50-meter) Daibutsuden Hall, which houses an equally famed 49-foot-tall (15-meter) bronze statue of Buddha. Even today, it's an awe-inspiring structure, but one can only imagine the impact it would have had on visitors in Nara's heyday.

Away from the park, south of Kintetsu Station, the Nara-machi area, with its narrow streets lined with old wooden houses, is home to a mixture of galleries, places to eat and drink, and stores and workshops where you can discover centuries-old local crafts like *Nara shikki* lacquerware, *Nara ningyo* dolls, *Nara sarashi* cloth, *Nara akahada yaki* pottery, *Nara sumi* ink, and (yes, this one starts with Nara, too) *Nara fude* calligraphy brushes—all great and distinctive souvenirs.

RIGHT Nara's streets are filled with shops, like this one selling sweets, perfect for souvenirs.

ABOVE Todaiji's 49-foot-tall (15-meter) Daibutsu statue dates to the mid-700s, and has had to be patched up many times over the years, including after a ninth-century earthquake that temporarily decapitated him.

Japan's Dynamic Commercial City

On the face of it Japan's second city looks much like any other part of built-up urban Japan, but beyond the usual swathes of concrete and crowded streets there's something quite different about Osaka. First, there are Osakans, who have a reputation for being more direct, chatty, and open than is the norm in Japan. Then there's the energy, which no matter where you go in the center of the city never threatens to abate. And, of course, the food—Osaka is known as "Japan's kitchen". A trip here straight after Kyoto or Nara is like being on a different planet.

LEFT Osaka's street food includes *takoyaki*, battered octopus balls with a thick Worcestershire-like sauce, mayo and fish flakes; and *oden*, a winter dish with boiled eggs, daikon, *konnyaku* root, and fish cake in a soy-flavored *dashi*-rich broth.

Visit the neon-drenched Dotombori area, awash with bars and restaurants, and you get bombarded with all of Osaka's hustle and attitude; it's the perfect place for finding a rough and ready place to sample Osaka's signature dish—a kind of thick, savory pancake combining vegetables, seafood and/or meat called *okonomiyaki*. East of there is where Osaka does its Akihabara impersonation with Den Den Town, the place to hunt for home electronics and things geeky, while just to the north you get America-mura, a lively shopping area full of boutiques catering to teens and twenty-somethings.

LEFT The Shinsekai area, easily recognizable because of the giant *fugu* (blowfish) signs and the Tsutenkaku Tower, teems with restaurants. It's especially known for *kushiage*, skewers of battered and deep-fried meat, seafood and vegetables.
RIGHT With the large crab hanging outside, Kani Doraku restaurants are easy to spot, and great places to try local seafood.
BELOW LEFT Osaka's central wholesale market provides the city with super-fresh, high-quality seafood.

Continuing the all-about-now theme, Osaka's western waterfront is home to one of Japan's coolest family days out, with Kaiyukan, the world's largest aquarium, as well as Kansai's answer to Tokyo Disney, the Universal Studios amusement park. The latter pulls in almost thirteen million visitors a year with many of the same white-knuckle and high-tech attractions found in its American sister parks, plus Japan-only attractions that includes a *kawaii*-soaked Hello Kitty parade—magical

ABOVE Universal Studios Japan rivals Disney in Tokyo as Japan's top amusement park.
LEFT The Kaiyukan aquarium. Along with the nearby Universal Studios Japan, it's one of Osaka's best family attractions.
OPPOSITE PAGE BOTTOM The Dotombori area is at the heart of Osaka's nightlife and with the iconic neon Glico man sign is also one of the city's most photographed spots.

for anyone into the super cute, but the kind of thing that could drive others to drink.

What about Osaka's history? Osaka doesn't tend to wear its past quite as conspicuously as say Kyoto or Nara. You can forget about searching for picturesque geisha districts here, and you'll want to save the Zen experiences for elsewhere. That said, there are some remnants of old Japan that can't be overlooked and Osaka Castle is certainly one of them. Besides being an impressive sight in its own right, the eight-story castle, first built by feudal lord Toyotomi Hideyoshi in 1585 but now dating from 1931, gives great views across Osaka and with its collection of feudal artifacts and other historic exhibits provides insights into Osaka's samurai past. You can catch other glimpses of the past in shrines like Tenmangu, which was founded in the tenth century and is now the site of a major annual summer festival that features a procession of floats on land and a flotilla

of lantern-lit boats on the canal, as well as the country's oldest temple, Shitennoji, which was founded in the 600s by the same prince who established Nara's first temples and still boasts an unusual stone *torii* gateway said to date to the 1200s.

After Osaka, the thought of visiting another major city might not appeal to everyone, but Kobe—the now resurgent port city devastated by a magnitude 7.3 earthquake in 1995—is just twenty-five minutes away by train, and a popular trip. The main attraction is the city's mix of old and new, East and West, which reflects its key role in the opening up of Japan in the latter part of the 1800s. Looking to the past, there's the Kitano-cho district and its nineteenth-century Western-style architecture, plus a lively Chinatown, both of which can trace their roots to early foreign influences in Meiji-era Japan. With the Harbor Land redevelopment, some of that past has also been dragged into the

TOP RIGHT Osaka Castle occupies a vast space in central Osaka, with land that reflects seasonal changes.
ABOVE The main donjon of Osaka Castle
TOP LEFT The Tenjin Matsuri in late July is one of Japan's three greatest festivals. With a thousand-year history, today it sees lively parades of portable shrines, fireworks, a lantern-lit flotilla, and more.

RIGHT Kobe port at night. On the left is the 354-foot (108-meter) Kobe Port Tower, which features a revolving café at its top and an observation deck that provides stunning city and port views.
BELOW Kobe is home to one of Japan's three Chinatowns.

present, where renovated brick warehouses form the focal point of a shopping and dining area. And also in the bay area come the manmade Port Island and Rokko Island, home to attractions like the futuristic looking Kobe Fashion Museum, a flower and bird park, and the Kobe Science Museum.

Of course, there's also Kobe beef, or *Kobe-gyu* to use the Japanese term. To be fair, there are great beef brands all over Japan—and you could make a case for many being as good as *Kobe-gyu*—it's just that no other wagyu has the international brand recognition of Kobe's legendary beef, thanks to the tales of how the cows are pampered and raised, and how the meat simply melts in the mouth. If you are going to splurge and try it, Kobe is the place.

RIGHT The Kitano-cho district of Kobe is known for its late Meiji-era Western-style architecture.
BELOW AND BELOW RIGHT *Kobe-gyu* is among Japan's finest beef brands and comes with a price to match.

Home of the Archetypal Japanese Castle

Fans of the Sean Connery incarnation of James Bond might well recognize Himeji's main attraction—its castle—from its appearance in *You Only Live Twice*, a film in which Bond not only managed to slap on a bit of boot polish and pass himself off as a Japanese fisherman with a heavily accented *konnichiwa*, but where the underbelly of Himeji Castle was home to the Japanese Secret Service's ninja training school.

ABOVE Manhole cover design has been raised to an art form in Japan, each local area having designs that reflect its heritage and traditions. The herons here are a nod to Himeji Castle's nickname, Hakuro-jo.

While the ninja training school sadly doesn't exist (although, if it did, would we really know?), Himeji Castle is nonetheless a magnificent place to visit. Arguably Japan's finest castle, it was originally built in the mid-fourteenth century but over the following three centuries went through several restorations and expansions to become an impenetrable behemoth of a structure. At its peak it had three moats, eighty-four gateways and a web of tight, meandering passages designed to tire and confuse attackers while defenders could pick them off with arrows through the thousand "loophole" windows.

ABOVE The castle's interiors are modern reconstructions but give a sense of traditional design and construction methods.
TOP RIGHT The view from the castle's upper levels.
RIGHT There are no guards on duty at Himeji, but that doesn't stop some people from dressing up.

LEFT A view of Kokoen Garden next to the castle. Despite the classical appearance, the nine separate gardens were actually built in the 1990s, although they are no less beautiful for it.
OPPOSITE PAGE, BOTTOM Himeji Castle. The castle and nearby gardens are a wonderful sight year-round, but there's something extra special when the cherry blossoms briefly bloom in late March or early April.

Today Himeji Castle still boasts a five-story main tower, three smaller donjons and numerous keeps and turrets that, thanks to their distinctive white plastering, gray roof tiles and overall shape, have brought the castle the nickname Hakuro-jo (White Heron Castle)—seen from the correct angle it really does resemble a heron spreading its wings.

Beyond the castle, there are other reasons to take a day trip to Himeji from Kobe (thirty-one miles or fifty kilometers) or Osaka (fifty-six miles or ninety kilometers). Next to Himeji Castle is the Kokoen Garden, consisting of nine separate gardens, constructed in the early 1990s but designed in the Edo-era style, offering a fine example of Japanese landscaping. And an easy walk from there are two more relatively new additions to the city, this time designed by two of Japan's most lauded contemporary architects. The first is the Museum of Literature, designed by Tadao Ando (the man also behind Omotesando Hills in Tokyo and many of the galleries on Naoshima Island), a slick blend of rough concrete, water features and angular patterns. The second is the Kenzo Tange-designed Hyogo Prefectural Museum of History, a minimalist classic, featuring concrete and glass cubes.

A Mountain-top Pilgrimage Center

As the birthplace of Shingon Buddhism, pilgrims have been traveling to Koyasan in Wakayama Prefecture for centuries, taking to the cypress-clad mountain and the small town that shares its name to pay their respects at the mausoleum of the Buddhist monk Kobo Daishi, who founded the Shingon sect here in 816 AD. Wandering among the towering trees and ancient, mossy cemetery that now stretches from his resting place, it's not hard to see why Kobo Daishi settled on this site for his temple after returning from years of studying Buddhism in China.

The cemetery, called Okunoin, is both vast and mystical, many of its tombstones and statues almost reclaimed by nature, while the main hall near Kobo's off-limits tomb emits an otherworldly charm, ten thousand constantly lit lanterns combining with the scent of incense and occasional droning sound of chanting. Even among Japan's much-vaunted collection of World Heritage Sites, Okunoin makes Koyasan a standout.

But it isn't the be all and end all of a trip to Kobo Daishi's holy mountain. The mountain's accommodation draws in pilgrims and non-pilgrims alike for the chance to experience (to a degree at least)

RIGHT The Garan, Koyasan's central temple complex, is one of several important Shingon Buddhist structures on the mountain. Others include Kongobuji Temple, home to a picturesque raked-sand garden and one of Japan's finest collections of screen paintings.

life as a monk. Some fifty of the 120 small monasteries on and around Koyasan provide what's called *shukubo* (paid temple lodgings), which although not Spartan (there's no sleeping on beds of nails) is typically far from the luxury one might expect at a traditional Japanese inn. Accommodation-wise, what you get is a simple, small tatami-mat room with just a futon and perhaps a TV and a small table. What makes a night at a *shukubo* special, other than the kind of peace and quiet that can make your ears ring, is the carefully presented multi-course dinner of *shojin ryori*, the vegetarian cuisine featuring tofu and seasonal vegetables eaten by the monks. Capping that, many of the

ABOVE AND LEFT You could easily lose yourself for hours in Okunoin cemetery, looking at the moss-covered tombstones and the child-like *Jizo* statues. It can be eerie in places, a little odd in others—some companies and former business people have tombs here with small post boxes where you can leave your name card after paying your respects.

monasteries also allow guests to take part in certain daily monastery rituals; usually the early-morning prayer session and (depending on the monastery) the morning fire ceremony that follows, where against a backdrop of unrelenting drumbeat and chanting, you watch a lone monk burning 108 small pieces of wood to represent the 108 defilements that must be overcome before reaching enlightenment.

ABOVE A side trip from Koyasan, this UNESCO World Heritage-designated Seigantoji Temple near the Nachi Falls features striking Momoyoma-style architecture.
LEFT The morning fire ceremony is open to guests at most temple lodgings and is well worth an early alarm.
FAR LEFT The *shojin ryori* served at Koyasan's temple lodgings is fully vegetarian, using in-season local produce and tofu (served alongside rice and pickles) to create an array of visually stunning and sublimely flavored dishes. One local specialty you will be served is *koya-dofu*, a rehydrated freeze-dried tofu (originally dried outside in the frigid winter air here) that oozes a savory *dashi* stock when you bite down on it.

CHAPTER 4

WESTERN HONSHU AND SHIKOKU ISLAND

Daishoin Temple, Miyajima

Hiroshima Peace Memorial

Tokushima Awa Odori Festival

Ritsurin Garden

INTRODUCING WESTERN HONSHU AND SHIKOKU

Moving west from Kyoto, Nara and the rest of the Kansai region, Japan's tourist trail gets a little less worn—at least by overseas travelers—but that isn't to say the west is devoid of attractions. In the western part of Honshu island is one of Japan's most famous and undoubtedly most moving destinations; Hiroshima and the Peace Park that stands as a harrowing testament to the horrors of nuclear war. Nearby comes the famous floating shrine on Miyajima Island, while elsewhere in the Seto Inland Sea, which separates Honshu from another of Japan's four main islands, Shikoku, are other islands like the contemporary art haven of Naoshima. Then comes Shikoku itself, a largely rural, slow-moving part of Japan that is known as the site of an eighty-eight-temple pilgrimage.

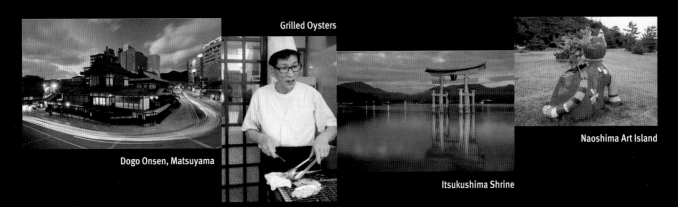

Grilled Oysters

Dogo Onsen, Matsuyama

Itsukushima Shrine

Naoshima Art Island

A Memorial to Tragedy and a Beacon of Hope

On the morning of August 6, 1945, a 9,700-pound (4, 400-kilogram) nuclear bomb was dropped on Hiroshima from the B-29 Superfortress bomber the Enola Gay and the world would for the first time witness the full extent of both the power and horror of nuclear armament. In the moment the bomb detonated just above the streets of central Hiroshima, eighty thousand men, women and children lost their lives in a single instance. In the weeks that followed, another sixty thousand of Hiroshima's residents would die of injuries and radiation sickness. Three days later, another bomb was dropped on the city of Nagasaki, eventually claiming an estimated eighty thousand more victims. The war in the Pacific was over, but at what cost of innocence.

Situated in Hiroshima's Peace Memorial Park, the skeletal frame of the former Hiroshima Prefectural Industrial Promotion Hall, otherwise known as the Gembaku Dome (an abbreviated form of "nuclear-bomb dome"), has become a global symbol of the tragedy of August 6, a warning of the potential manmade Armageddon created by the weaponization of nuclear power. Yet in a city where some two-thirds of the buildings were destroyed in the initial explosion and resulting fires, the fact that the dome survived, despite being located right at the hypocenter of the explosion, also gave Japan a symbol of hope; a hope that was echoed in the amazing postwar recovery of not just Japan, but with Hiroshima once again becoming a bustling, prosperous city.

Hope aside, it is, however, impossible not to feel moved by a visit to Hiroshima's peace park. The Children's Peace

ABOVE The exhibits in the Peace Memorial Museum depict the horror of the immediate aftermath of the A-bomb.
RIGHT The Children's Peace Monument. Schoolchildren from Japan and overseas send origami cranes to be displayed in glass cases around the monument, a lasting tradition in memory of those who lost their lives in nuclear war.

TOP Once a local government office, the Gembaku Dome has become the symbol of Hiroshima's tragic past.

Monument in particular is hard to digest. This 30-foot-high (nine-meter) domed pedestal featuring the bronze statue of a child holding a paper crane, was built in memory of Sadako Sasaki, a leukemia patient who hoped she might recover if she

could fold a thousand origami cranes (a symbol of good health and longevity in Japan). Sadako died aged twelve in 1955, without ever folding her thousandth crane, but her classmates kept making cranes for her, as do children all over Japan and beyond today. Maybe there's hope in that, too.

Of course, Hiroshima has more to it than its tragic past. The castle here (a rebuild) is an attractive reminder of its former feudal strength, while the city's postwar growth is testament to its drive to not let the past define its future. In entertainment districts like Nagarekawa, you find lively bars and nightspots, and around the city there are numerous places to sample Hiroshima's culinary contributions to Japan, whether that's its version of *okonomiyaki* pancakes or its famed oysters. There's sport, too—and there's no better place to soak up Hiroshima's energy than at a Carp ballgame.

The Famous Itsukushima "Floating" Torii Gate

Some place names tell you almost everything you need to know about a destination, and Miyajima—literally, "shrine island"—near the city of Hiroshima is most definitely one of them. The roughly six-by two-mile (nine- by four-kilometer) island, separated from mainland Hiroshima Prefecture by a ten-minute ferry ride across a 1,640-foot (500-meter) wide strip of water called the Onoseto Strait, is famed for being home to one of Japan's most distinctive Shinto sights—the "floating" *torii* gateway at Itsukushima Shrine.

It's said there has been a shrine in some form or other on the island since the late sixth century, with the 55-foot (16.8-meter) *torii* gateway itself, which now dates to 1875, first being built into the bay in 1168. The towering vermilion-colored *torii* is not the only of the shrine's buildings built over the water, but the image of the *torii* when the tide is in and it appears to be floating has become one of Japan's most

ABOVE The rice scoop (*shamoji*, but *shakushi* in Miyajima) is in every home in Japan. It was first created by a monk on Miyajima several hundred years ago, which is why you'll find *ema* (votive plaques) shaped like them on the island. The world's largest scoop is on display on the main shopping street—Omotesando (not to be confused with the very different Tokyo boulevard).

TOP Miyajima's "floating" *torii* gate is one of Japan's most iconic sights when the tide is in, so make sure you time a visit right or you get it looking like this—good, but not "wow". Hotels in the area can tell travelers the best tide times.
TOP Pilgrims visit Miyajima from all over Japan on festival days.
LEFT Grilled oysters are a popular snack you can pick up on Miyajima's main shopping street.

recognizable sights alongside Mount Fuji, Kinkakuji Temple in Kyoto and Kamakura's giant statue of Buddha. The only potential disappointment for visitors is if they turn up when the tide is out and the *torii* is poking out of mucky silt—not quite as impressive!

Shrine aside, like the other three thousand or so mostly tiny islands in the Inland Sea, Miyajima also boasts some stunning natural beauty, in particular the hiking trails that wind through the forested Mount Misen and end with sweeping views across the island and toward Hiroshima Bay and the Inland Sea. The shrine also isn't the only historic attraction on Miyajima. As well as Shintoism, Buddhism has left an impressive mark in the shape of the twelfth-century Daishoin Temple, which for centuries flourished under imperial patronage. Then there's the old Machiya-dori, a street lined with atmospheric wooden *machiya* houses that create a very old-world feel, even though many of them now house contemporary art galleries, plush inns, and shops.

ABOVE Sutra bells at Daishoin Temple. Dating to the twelfth century and closely linked to the imperial family until the nineteenth century, Daishoin is the main Shingon-sect temple in Western Japan.
ABOVE LEFT The pathways at Daishoin are lined with hundreds of small *Jizo* statues, often wearing red and white knitted caps given by visitors.
LEFT Itsukushima Shrine, with its five-story pagoda, is gorgeous when illuminated at night.

Islands in the Sun

Stretching some 280 miles (450 kilometers) east to west and separating Honshu, Shikoku and Kyushu (three of Japan's four main islands), the Seto Inland Sea and its three thousand or so small islands combine a diverse range of attractions with stunning, sun-kissed natural beauty. From contemporary art projects to sleek island retreats and traditional ways of life, there's something for everyone here.

For contemporary art fans, the islands are probably best known for Naoshima, once a sleepy fishing island that began an incredible transformation in the 1990s as the focal point of publishing company Benesse's innovative art project, Benesse Art Site Naoshima. Now dubbed "Art Island" by some, Naoshima's makeover started with the Tadao Ando-designed Benesse House, a sleek combination of beachfront hotel and gallery that houses work by artists like Warhol and Hockney, but more impressively has a collection of outdoor installations spread about the beach and cliffs around it.

Benesse didn't stop there. Next came the Art House Project in the village of Honmura, where a handful of old houses, as well as a temple and a shrine, have been turned into permanent art installations. Naoshima's art then expanded further with a gallery dedicated to Korean artist Lee Ufan and another Tadao Ando-designed gallery called the Chichu Art Museum that is home to work by Claude Monet.

Very different from Naoshima is the nearby, but larger Shodoshima. While the two islands share a Mediterranean-like climate and coastline that can be both rugged and exquisitely picturesque, that's about all they have in common. For the Japanese, Shodoshima is known for its

BELOW Benesse House, comprising a hotel and a museum, was designed by Tadao Ando to blend in with the Setonaikai National Park that surrounds it. **BELOW RIGHT** Four of Claude Monet's painted works from the *Water Lilies* collection are exhibited at the Chichu Art Museum.

soy-sauce production (there are several factories large and very small that can be visited) and for being where olives were first cultivated in Japan. The olive groves and olive-infused spa baths at Olive Park—yes, an olive-themed park—are one of the island's main attractions.

The smaller islands in the area are worth exploring, too. Both Megijima and Ogijima host Art Site venues that are worth the short ferry trips from Takamatsu in their own right, but they also combine it with a lovely "old island" feel. On Megijima, as well as art, there are former smuggler's caves to explore and folkloric tales of ogres to hear about, while on

Ogijima, you can soak up small, idyllic island life by exploring the maze of narrow, winding streets hugging the main hill, every so often coming across a cat basking in the sun, vegetable patches, wild flowers reclaiming pavement, or an old building transformed on the inside by art. It blends together so well, old and the new without a hint of conflict.

ABOVE The port on Shodoshima Island harks back to an older age. **LEFT** Shodoshima's Olive Park celebrates the island being the first place in Japan to grow olives. **BELOW AND BOTTOM** The art island of Naoshima features the *Yellow Pumpkin* and *Red Pumpkin* by renowned artist Yayoi Kusama.

ABOVE Thousands of sunbaked islands dot the Inland Sea, offering a mix of local tradition, stunning scenery and (more recently) unforgettable art venues. **RIGHT** It is actually possible to bathe at the Naoshima Bath *I Love Yu*, an art facility designed by artist Shinro Ohtake.

A Pilgrimage to Japan's "Other" Island

Shikoku, the smallest and least populated of Japan's four main islands, has been attracting pilgrims for more than a thousand years. Called *o-henro-san* in Japanese, they come for a 870-mile (1,400-kilometer) tour that takes in eighty-eight temples associated with the Buddhist monk Kobo Daishi, who founded the Shingon sect of Buddhism in Koyasan (site of the only of the eighty-eight temples not in Shikoku) in the ninth century. Admittedly, the typical *o-henro-san* nowadays isn't walking or taking in the entire route, but on any visit to Shikoku you are very likely to see them with their distinctive white jackets and slacks, conical straw hat, rosary beads, sutra book, bell and wooden staff—and all the while they will be dropping a small fortune on transportation, accommodation, souvenirs and, of course, temple donations.

Not that you have to be a pilgrim to enjoy Shikoku; from rural and rugged to cosmopolitan, the island contains a great variety of places to explore beyond temples. The main city, Matsuyama, has a very relaxed provincial air to it, great seafood and sake, and a rich history that includes the magnificent Matsuyama Castle, initially built in its all-encompassing hilltop position in the seventeenth century by warlord Yoshiaki Kato. It's a tough climb to reach the gates to the three-story donjon (one that would have been brutal in full battle gear, though there is a cable car option these days), but inside you get rewarded with sweeping views over Matsuyama and Shikoku's northwest coast, as well as a fine collection of such things as weaponry, scrolls and banners.

TOP RIGHT A pilgrim visits Ishiteji Temple in Dogo. One of the most distinctive of the eighty-eight temples on the pilgrimage because of a mix of architectural styles (there's even a golden mandala here), it offers a "cheat" version of the pilgrimage with eighty-eight bags of soil (one from each temple) arranged outside a small hall. Walk around it once touching each bag and you are done. Easy.

LEFT AND BELOW
Matsuyama Castle is a mighty structure. Dominating Matsuyama's central skyline, it provides great inland and ocean views.

ABOVE LEFT AND RIGHT
The Dogo Onsen Honkan is a beautiful structure. The baths inside are relatively small, but they have a classic grace to them, with some Hokusai artwork on the wall. If you visit, be sure to pay extra to visit a past Emperor's private rooms here—he even had a lacquered toilet.

Hop on one of Matsuyama's streetcars and head a couple of kilometers to the Dogo Onsen hot-spring area and you'll see a very different part of Shikoku. This is the oldest recognized hot spring in Japan, with bathing here detailed in the 1,300-year-old classic history book, *Chronicles of Japan*. While lots of traditional inns in the area have their own natural hot spring baths (as is common with Japanese inns), the focal point in Dogo is the public baths at the Dogo Onsen Honkan, a three-story wooden structure built in 1894 that was the inspiration for the bathhouse in Hayao Miyazaki's Oscar-winning animated film *Spirited Away*. Meiji-era novelist Natsume Soseki, regarded as modern Japan's preeminent writer, also became a fan of the baths during his time as a teacher in Matsuyama—in his book *Botchan*, this is where the eponymous main character comes to bathe.

And Soseki isn't Matsuyama's only literary figure, the city is the birthplace of Masaoka Shiki (1867–1902), one of Japan's

great haiku masters, and a close friend of Soseki. Haiku poetry culture runs deep in the city, which now brands itself as the "city of haiku" and runs annual international haiku competitions. Scattered around the city are ninety-two haiku postboxes where visitors can pick up cards, write haiku and post them to the city, while the local tourism office runs haiku walking and writing tours in English. There are even haiku bars—like Hoyaken and Riff—where you can write and share haiku (in English as well as Japanese) over sake and cocktails; an unusually creative tourism initiative by Japanese standards.

To the east, on the opposite side of Shikoku, Takamatsu is worth noting, too, first for its beautiful and sprawling Ritsurin

Garden, but also as the place to catch a ferry to islands like Naoshima and Shodoshima (pages 102-103). More central, another place that can't be ignored is the city of Tokushima, home to Japan's most vibrant summer festival, the ancient Awa Odori. Over three days in August, the event, which can trace its roots back to the 1100s, sees in excess of a million onlookers and 100,000 dancers kicking up a noisy, colorful storm throughout the streets of Tokushima.

RIGHT AND ABOVE In the heart of Shikoku, the remote Iya Valley is famous for its stunning gorges, thatched cottages and slow rural pace. It's also got historic vine bridges like these here, which sway just enough to get the heart racing.

BELOW Konpira Shrine, located on the wooded Mount Zozu, is reached by 1,368 stone steps. For that imperial feeling, you can actually hire a palanquin to carry you all the way to the top.

CHAPTER 5
KYUSHU
AND OKINAWA

Kyushu

50 km
50 miles

N

Tsushima

Hibiki-nada

Ko-saki

Higashi-suido

Iki-suido

Iki-Shima
Iki

Genkai-nada

Yamaguchi
Iwakuni
Kurahashijima

Shimonoseki
Ogori
Shunan
Kudamatsu
Hikari
Yanai
Yashirojima
Imaba

Kitakyushu
Nakama
Kokura
Ube
Yukuhashi
Hofu
Nagashima
Matsuyama

Muna Kata

Fukuoka Int'l Airport

Shikano-shima

Hukutsu
Iizuka
Tagawa
Suo-nada
Hime-shima
Kunimi
Kunisaki
Iyo-nada
Iyo

Fukuoka
Itoshima
Nanzoin Temple, Dazaifu Tenmangu Shrine

Madara-shima
Tenmangu
Dazaifu
Chikushino
Buzen
Usa
Bungotakada
Kitsuki
Nagahama
Yawatahama
Uchiko
Ozu

Fukuoka Castle, Canal City Mall, Hakata Port, Sleeping Buddha (Nanzoin Temple)
Ogori
Ukiha
Hita
Beppu Hot Spring Pools, Takegawara Spa
Beppu-wan
Sada-misaki
Seiyo
S H I K O K

Azuchi-O-shima
Taku-shima
Ikitsuki-shima
Watada
Tosu
Kurume
Chikugo

Uku-jima
Hirado-shima
Hirado
Matsuura
Saza
Imari
Saga
Shofukuji Temple
Yame
K Y U S H U
Oita
Beppu
Hoyasu-seto (Hoyo-kaikyo)
Yoshida
Kihoku
Uwa-kai
Uwajima-wan
Uwajima

Ojika-jima
Ojika
Sasebo
Yanagawa
Omuta
Yamaga
Aso
Inukai
Usuki
Tsukumi
Ainan
Shimanto

Goto-Retto
Shin-kamigoto
Nakadori-jima
Huis Ten Bosch
Kawatana
Ureshino
Arao
Tamana
Kikuchi
Ogumi
Bungo-ono
Saiki
Sen-zaki
Tsurumi-zaki
Bungo-suido
Sukumo
Tosashima

Narao
Omura
Isahaya
Ariake-kai
Uekei
Takeda
Kamae Oaza

Fukue-jima
Kaba-shima
Shimabara Castle
Nagasaki Peace Park, Peace Museum, Chinatown, Dejima Reconstruction, Glover Garden
Nagasaki
Obama
Shimabara
Kumamoto
Uto
Kosa
Takachiho
Kitagawa
Nobeoka
Oki-no-shima

Goto
Ose-zaki
Unzen
Shimabara-wan
Mifune
Marotsuka

Danjo-gunto
Minami-Shimabara
Reihoku
Kamia masuka
Yatsushiro
Itsuki
Shiiba
Misato
Togo
Hyuga

Amakusa-nada
Amakusa
Ashikita
Tagari
Nishimera
Kijo
Saito

Shimo-shima
Minamata
Hitoyoshi
Nishiki
Hyuga-nada

Naga-shima
Izumi
Isa
Ebino
Kobayashi

Akune
Yusui
Saito

Kami-koshiki-jima
Satsuma
Kobayashi

Naka-koshiki-jima
Satsuma Sendai
Aira
Kamo
Kajiki
Kirishima
Miyakonojo
Miyazaki

Shimo-koshiki-jima
Ichiki-Kushikino
Nichinan

Koshikijima-Retto
Kagoshima
Shibushi

Koshiki-kaikyo
Minami-Satsuma
Tarumizu
Kushima

Noma-mizaki
Minami-Kyushu
Kiirecho
Kanoya
Shibushi-won

Bonotsu
Makurazaki
Toi-misaki

Bono-misaki
Ibusuki
Ikeda-ko
Yamakawa

Sata

Kuroshima

Sata
Sata-misaki

Mishima

Okinawa

Ocean Expo Park, Okinawa Churaumi Aquarium

Okinawa Hont

Nago

Cape Manzamo

Ryukyu-Mura

Uruma

PACIFIC OCEA

Nakagusuku Castle

Naha
Tsuboya Pottery District, Shuri Castle, Kosetsu Ichiba Food Market, Eisa Dancing, Kokusai-dori

Zamami-jima

Aharen Beach, Tokashiki Island

Okinawa World

Itoman
Okinawa Peace Memorial Museum, Himeyuri-no-to

N

20 km
10 miles

Yaeyama Islands

Irabu-jima
Hirara

Minna-jima
Miyako-jima

Yaeyama Islands
Tarama-jima

Kabira Bay

Ishigaki-jima
Taketomi Island

Iriomote-jima
Ishigaki

Nakanougan-jima

Hateruma-jima

N

50 km
25 miles

Kuroshima

Kuchinoerabu

Ancient Cedars

Yakushima

Okinawa Churaumi Aquarium

Daizafu Tenmangu Shrine, Fukuoka

Kannawa Steam Bath

Aharen Beach, Tokashiki Island

INTRODUCING KYUSHU AND OKINAWA

Japan's far west and far south have a vibe all of their own. From cities like cosmopolitan Fukuoka and historic Nagasaki—the latter indelibly marked by the horror of nuclear war—through to the incredible ecology and diversity of Yakushima Island in Kyushu and the island cultures and subtropical scenery of Okinawa, these far reaches of Japan offer up a tapestry of experiences and sights quite unlike anywhere else.

Shuri Castle, Naha

Shop near Daizafu Tenmangu

Ishigaki Island

Yakushima Island

A Regional City on the Rise

With a growing population approaching 1.5 million and an average age (thirty-eight) that makes it one of the youngest cities in a country facing a major aging crisis, Fukuoka is one of those rare regional cities in Japan that's on the rise. Hakata Port and Fukuoka Airport have made the city a regional transport hub, while the service sector industry, IT, logistics and high-tech manufacturing have also made Fukuoka the region's economic center. And the city certainly has a youthful energy to go along with that, whether that's in the three thousand bars, clubs and restaurants of the lively Nakasu district or in modern developments like the Canal City Hakata mall, which (though admittedly not quite Tokyo Midtown) has six floors of stores selling everything from the latest fashions to toys and games, not to mention restaurants, a thirteen-screen cinema complex, and a traditional theater.

That doesn't mean that Fukuoka isn't proud of its roots. It is, and those roots run deep. The ports here were active at least as far back as the sixth century and then saw a spurt of development in the twelfth century when what's now Fukuoka (then it was called Hakata) became the official hub for trade and communication with China. It was at this time that Shofukuji Temple (Japan's first Zen temple) was founded, four hundred years before the city's other remaining historical landmark, the Edo-era Fukuoka Castle.

LEFT Canal City Hakata, Fukuoka's main shopping and entertainment complex.
RIGHT The sleeping Buddha at Nanzoin Temple. At 134 feet (41 meters) in length, it is one of the world's largest bronze statues.
TOP RIGHT Hakata Port, around which the city has flourished.
ABOVE MIDDLE Love locks have become a "thing" at Fukuoka Tower. It tells you something about the nature of Japan that even these are neatly arranged.

More than anything, however, you can't have a conversation about Fukuoka without mentioning the food. In a country with something of a noodle obsession, the local variety of ramen—Hakata ramen—is considered by many to be the finest example of Japan's favorite feel-good food thanks to its combination of rich, milky, pork-bone broth and thin but slightly chewy noodles topped with slices of roast pork and flavorings that range from sesame seeds and crushed garlic to pickled ginger. There's no shortage of ramen restaurants around Fukuoka (or around any part of Japan for that matter), but the most enjoyable way to try Hakata ramen is at one of the many *yatai* (outdoor food stalls) in the city. Another of Fukuoka's culinary signatures, the 150 or so *yatai* here are small affairs typically specializing in a single cuisine (be that ramen or *oden* or *yakitori*) with a dozen or half a dozen shoulder-to-shoulder counter seats surrounding the cooking area that makes it impossible not to strike up a conversation.

TOP AND ABOVE Fukuoka locals will tell you they have the best street food in Japan, and it's hard to disagree. As well as casual *yatai* food stalls all around the city, Fukuoka is the birthplace of Hakata ramen (Hakata being the old name for the region), which is so revered by ramen fans across Japan that they travel to Fukuoka just for the noodles.

ABOVE One of Japan's six major sumo tournaments is held in Fukuoka over fifteen days in the second half of November every year. Tickets for the cheaper seats can be picked up on the day itself and the spectacle—pomp and power included—is quite something.
RIGHT Not in Fukuoka city, but Kitakyushu city to the northeast, in late April to early May the wisteria tunnels at Kawachi Fuji Garden are well worth a half day trip.

Japan's Historic Southern Port and Second Atomic Bomb Site

In the early hours of August 9, 1945, three days after the nuclear bombing of Hiroshima, the B-29 bomber Bockscar, accompanied by four reconnaissance and measurement planes, set off on a mission to drop a second, larger nuclear device on the industrial city of Kokura. With cloud coverage and smoke from previous conventional bombing raids making it impossible to properly identify their target, however, Kokura was spared, and with fuel running low attention turned to the mission's secondary target, the munitions factories at Nagasaki. The result was horrific, with an estimated thirty-five thousand people dying as a result of the blast and another sixty thousand injured. The Mitsubishi munitions works were destroyed, but so too was half of Nagasaki.

Like Hiroshima, which is now a thriving modern city, Nagasaki's postwar recovery has been remarkable. Yet also like Hiroshima, Nagasaki continues to honor its victims and warn of the horrors of nuclear armament. As a result, the city's Peace Park, the focal point of Nagasaki's nuclear remembrance, is one of the most sobering places you can visit in Japan; most obviously because of the harrowing imagery and exhibits at the Peace Museum, but so too because of the tragic stories behind many of the sculptures in the Peace Park. But not all of Nagasaki's past is tragic, and the city still gladly recalls its days as one of the four official points of contact between Japan and the outside world during the Edo era, when from 1633 to 1853 under the *sakoku* isolation policy, under pain of death no Japanese could leave Japan and no foreigner enter.

In Nagasaki's case, the city was where Japan traded with the Dutch, which explains why today Nagasaki is home to a Dutch theme park, complete with

windmills and tulips, called Huis Ten Bosch. Elsewhere in Nagasaki, you can also visit a reconstruction of Dejima, the once Dutch enclave and trading post, which gave limited access to the West and Western science and thinking to Japanese traders and scholars. While highlighting the influx of overseas culture that hit

Nagasaki when isolation came to an end are other historic sites like Glover Garden, the first Western-style house and garden built (by British trader Thomas Glover) in Japan, and Nagasaki's bustling Chinatown. It all combines to give Nagasaki a unique feel—a beguiling mix of old and new, vibrant and somber, East and West.

ABOVE Mount Inasa's (1,093 feet or 333 meters) observation platform, accessible by ropeway, provides the famed "Ten Million Dollar Night View" of the city. **LEFT** The Peace Statue by Seibo Kitamura is Nagasaki's most recognized monument to the A-bomb tragedy. **OPPOSITE PAGE, BOTTOM RIGHT** A two-hour train ride from Nagasaki, the five-tiered Shimabara castle is listed as one of the 100 Fine Castles of Japan by the Japan Castle Foundation.

Overseas influences can be seen all over Nagasaki, from the lively Chinatown (left) and Western structures like Glover Garden (right) to the Dutch-themed amusement park Huis Ten Bosch (top) with its windmills and tulip fields, a two-hour train ride from the city.

"Hell Pools" and Hot Sand Baths

Located in one of Japan's most geothermically active areas, it should be no surprise to hear that Beppu on Kyushu's eastern coast is known as Japan's premier hot spring and bathing resort town. Across Beppu are some three thousand springs that each day provide the many *onsen* baths and ryokan (traditional inns) of Beppu with approximately a hundred million liters of mineral-rich water ideal for soaking in—in the process, it's said, alleviating ailments as diverse as arthritis and piles. Like Hakone, Atami, and the other well known hot spring areas within easy reach of Tokyo, Kyushu's main hot spring resort provides a wonderful setting for experiencing a stay at a ryokan, a night away that typically includes not just a beautifully presented multi-course dinner and breakfast, but the chance to soak in a guests-only communal *onsen*, stay in a tatami-mat room, and relax (in traditional *yukata* gowns, if you fancy) in absolute peace and quiet.

ABOVE Warm mud baths—a popular beauty treatment for smoothing the skin.

ABOVE The Kamado Jigoku, literally "cooking pot hell", is one of the most attractive of Beppu's hell pools. Among the attractions here, visitors can drink the hot spring water (supposedly good for one's health) and enjoy hand and foot baths.

Unlike most resort towns, however, nature has given Beppu more than just bathing. The geothermal activity has also created varying-colored pools of boiling water and muds aptly called *jigoku* (hells). These eight *jigoku* in Beppu aren't for bathing (they are too hot for that), but are all popular attractions, each with their own distinguishing features. The Oniishibozu Jigoku in the Kannawa area of Beppu, for example, features thick, photogenic pools of bubbling gray mud, while in the same area the Umi Jigoku features a stunning blue pool of water and gardens with sub-pools that include a clear pond home to giant lotuses. Just as captivating is the Chinoike Jigoku (literally, the rather dramatic "Blood Pond Hell") in the Shibaseki district, which as the name suggests has boiling red waters. The underground activity has also been channeled into sand baths, a Beppu specialty that sees you buried up to your neck in 104-degree Fahrenheit (40-degree Celsius) sand for ten minutes with the promise (like bathing in the local water) of helping with ills as simple as fatigue and as complicated as digestion. How much it actually helps, who knows, but your skin comes out glowing and muscles very well pampered.

ABOVE Much like *onsen* waters, Beppu's hot-sand baths are said to help alleviate a range of muscle issues and minor ailments. They also leave the skin smooth and glowing.
RIGHT When you have so much steam naturally coming out of the earth, you might as well cook with it.

ABOVE The wonderfully named Chinoike Jigoku—"blood pond hell".
TOP LEFT You can actually see the earth at work when you look across Beppu, the steam rising from bathhouses and pools in one of Japan's most geothermally active areas.
TOP RIGHT Initially built in 1879, the Takegawara Spa is Beppu's most famous bath house, offering sand and regular baths.

A World Heritage Site of Unparalleled Natural Beauty

Of all Japan's World Heritage-designated sites, Yakushima Island, often mistaken as part of Okinawa but actually an almost-round blob (19 miles or 30 kilometers in diameter) on the map just south of Kyushu, really has nothing else in Japan it can be compared to. The island's fourteen thousand inhabitants get to live amid a natural beauty and diversity that is quite unlike anywhere else in Japan, the most famous aspect of which are the ancient *yaku-sugi* (cedars)—some estimated to be 7,200 years old—which reach upwards from the thick foliage that carpets the island's rugged peaks.

The forty or so of these peaks that measure in at over 3,280 feet (a thousand meters) have created a hiker's paradise, with trails that meander through mossy subtropical rainforest and over mountains streams, in the process taking in not only cedars that can reach 131 feet (40 meters) in height and a circumference of 32 feet (10 meters), but also a great variety of other flora and fauna that includes the Yakushima rhododendron, which speckles the island pink, white, and red in June. If that weren't enough, away from the interior, the rainforest then gives way to a coastline of pristine beaches and secluded offshore diving spots.

Make no mistake about it, however, Yakushima isn't an easy trip. While getting there is fairly straightforward (the island has an airport that connects to Osaka and Kagoshima, and the latter is also just two hours away by hydrofoil), the additional travel expenses can make for a costly holiday. On top of that, the environment itself can be hard, not just in the oppressively hot and humid summer months but because of the amount of rain that keeps the island so lush and beautiful. Yakushima averages some 32 feet of rain a year, which has led the locals to joke that they are the only place in the world to get 35 days of rain per month.

BELOW LEFT An array of flowers—some only found on this island—pepper Yakushima with color.
BELOW, OPPOSITE BOTTOM LEFT AND RIGHT A hike through Yakushima feels like a journey through a land time forgot. Gnarled tree roots reach outward like the fingers of ancient giants, moss coats rocks and rivers cut through the dense forest.

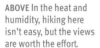

ABOVE In the heat and humidity, hiking here isn't easy, but the views are worth the effort.

TOP RIGHT Away from the interior, Yakushima's coastline has pretty beaches and diving opportunities. **RIGHT** The island's beauty is a natural habitat to a range of wildlife, some of which is endangered and only found here.

A Separate Island Culture and Sub-Tropical Holiday Resort

There's something magically different about Okinawa; something about the collection of seventy or so sub-tropical islands that makes them feel quite unlike (and proudly so) the rest of Japan. That's not entirely surprising given the climate, which even in February sees sunny daily highs reaching 68 degrees Fahrenheit (20 degrees Celsius) while Tokyo frequently shivers under grey skies, nor if you consider that until the 1870s the islands formed the independent Ryukyu Kingdom, and were then occupied for twenty-seven years by the U.S. after World War Two.

Naha, the main island's main city, is where most people start discovering the Ryukyus, exploring the main street Kokusai-dori, the colorful Kosetsu Ichiba food market and the Tsuboya pottery district, where the kilns churn out not just touristy statues of *shisa* lions but also fine ceramics. Even better, Naha is where visitors can first taste the difference between Okinawa and the rest of Japan, trying the local twist on soba noodles, *soki soba*, topped with melt-in-the-mouth rib meat, as well as *goya champuru* (a stir-fry of pork, egg, tofu and a bitter gourd called *goya*) and the unusual flavors of stewed *tonsoku* (pig's trotters) and *mimiga* (vinegared pig's ears).

ABOVE Kokusai-dori, the main street and entertainment district of Naha—a good place to search for restaurants and local flavors.
LEFT The outer wall of what remains of Shuri Castle.
OPPOSITE PAGE, BOTTOM LEFT *Goya champuru*, one of the classic Okinawan dishes, containing bitter gourd, a type of squash that is widely touted for its health benefits.
OPPOSITE PAGE, BELOW RIGHT Another Okinawan classic, *soki soba*, comes with soft belly pork or boneless pork ribs.

ABOVE The striking design of Shuri Castle. There's nothing else quite like it in Japan, but then again, this was once a separate kingdom.
LEFT A procession at the castle recalls the king and queen of Ryukyu.
RIGHT The massive gateway leading up to the castle.

Away from central Naha the rest of Okinawa-honto (*honto* meaning "main island") offers up numerous opportunities to learn about Okinawa's distant and near pasts. Once the capital of the Ryukyu Kingdom, the Shuri district of Naha is home to the main island's most historic site, Shuri Castle, which today includes a rebuilt limestone castle and its gardens (dating from 1992, but with some structures and relics dating to the 1500s). There's more Ryukyu heritage to explore

LEFT The scenic rock formations at Cape Manzamo. BELOW Okinawa is renowned for its water sports, but that's not the only way to get a buzz.

north of Naha, in sites such as Ryukyu Mura, which is home to preserved Okinawan farmhouses and also offers the chance to watch the local *eisa* dancing, while in a similar vein, Ocean Expo Park on the Motobu Peninsula covers local crafts and arts, as well as featuring a planetarium and one of Japan's leading aquariums, Okinawa Churaumi Aquarium.

The more recent history dates to Okinawa's bloody role in the final stages of World War Two, which saw approximately 140,000 Okinawans, 100,000 Japanese soldiers and thirteen thousand Americans losing their lives on the islands. An obvious remnant of the war and the postwar occupation are the twenty-five thousand US military personnel stationed in bases that account for eighteen percent of Okinawa's land mass, but there are also remnants that highlight the war's dreadful toll on Okinawa. Of all tales, none are as heartbreaking as that of Himeyuri-no-to, a deep pit at the southern tip of the island into which a group of high-school girls and their teachers jumped to their death rather than face the prospect of meeting the demonized invading US forces.

Beyond the Honto, there are many other islands to explore. And nowhere beats the collection of ten islands that make up the Yaeyama Islands 280 miles (450 kilometers) south of Naha. Some 1,243 miles (2,000 kilometers) from Tokyo—nearer to Taiwan than Naha—the Yaeyamas are both the southernmost and westernmost parts of Japan; so remote from the rest of the Japan that local Rykyuan languages are still spoken by some people here as well as Japanese. For most people who make it down this far south, the first stop is Ishigaki Island, the second largest of the Yaeyamas, and particularly famous in Japan for diving, water sports and the picturesque turquoise waters of Kabira Bay on its northern shore. Adding a very different experience to the Yaeyamas is the short boat trip from

ABOVE Kabira Bay on Ishigaki Island is one of the classic postcard images of Okinawa, with its white beaches, clear blue water and lush greenery.
LEFT There are plenty of ruins around the main island that reveal the old Ryukyu, like Nakagusuku Castle (pictured).

Ishigaki to Taketomi Island, where strict building regulations have left the tiny island defined by traditional red-roofed housing, stone walls and sandy roads along which water buffalo pull wooden carts-cum-taxis. A longer boat trip, 19 miles (30 kilometers) to Iriomote Island, brings the few visitors that venture this far to dense jungle and mangroves that provide the natural habitat for wildlife that includes the critically endangered (and extremely shy) Iriomote cat and a highly venomous pit viper.

ABOVE Tourists pose for a commemorative snap in traditional Ryukyu dress at Shuri Castle.
LEFT The Churaumi Aquarium in the north of the island. In the local dialect, *churaumi* means "beautiful sea", and for non-divers this is the best way to see exactly how beautiful the waters (and their inhabitants) around Okinawa are.

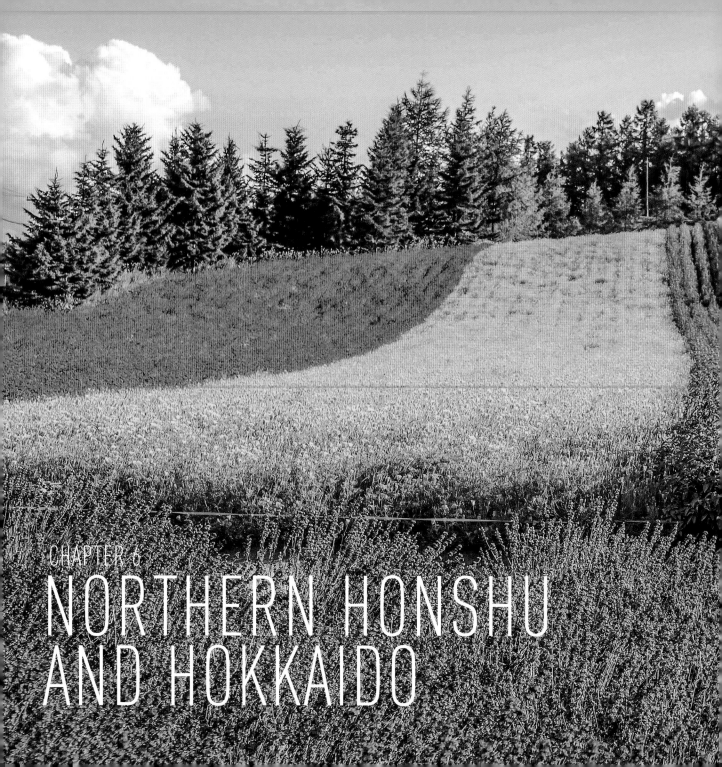

CHAPTER 6
NORTHERN HONSHU AND HOKKAIDO

Sapporo Snow Festival

Former Hokkaido Government Offices

Maguro-don (Tuna Rice Bowl)

Aomori Nebuta Festival

INTRODUCING NORTHERN JAPAN

Rugged, wild, harsh, rural, traditional, and touched by tragedy, Japan's north is many things. Beguiling, too. The north island of Hokkaido, only settled by the Japanese in the latter part of the 1800s (though the indigenous Ainu were there long before), is home to some of Japan's most remote and beautiful landscapes, as well as its finest winter sports destinations and a unique northern culture that has been shaped by long, hard winters. Then there's the Tohoku region in the northernmost reaches of Honshu, devastated in parts by the 2011 earthquake, tsunami and nuclear disaster, and though still facing a long road to recovery, a proud region full of rural charms, magical scenery, historical tales and centuries-old traditions.

Yamadera Temple

Otaru Canal

Skiing at Niseko

Red-Crowned Cranes

North from Tokyo to Sendai and Aomori

For people outside of Japan, it's likely that Tohoku will above all else be synonymous with the March 11, 2011 earthquake and tsunami and the nuclear disaster that followed. This 9.0 magnitude earthquake devastated much of Tohoku's eastern coast, destroying entire communities in parts of Iwate, Fukushima and Miyagi prefectures and claiming the lives of eighteen thousand people. More than five years on, the aftermath continues to unfold. Though infrastructure is returning and the debris has mostly been cleared, thousands still live in temporary housing and the local economy is in tatters. The crippled Fukushima nuclear plant has an exclusion zone around it and decades of treacherous decommissioning work ahead. Some communities will never be rebuilt, and almost-invisible issues like PTSD and other long-term mental health problems—it's estimated that one in three children in affected areas are suffering—mean many people in Tohoku are still very much in need of assistance.

Before the disaster, tourism—although Tohoku never attracted numbers like Tokyo or Kyoto or even other rural areas—was a gradually growing industry in the region, and it's tourism that many hope will help to rebuild the Tohoku economy. Even for just a long weekend away from Tokyo, the region certainly has lots to offer.

Take the bullet train up to Tohoku's largest city, Sendai, and you have a great base for exploring. For starters, you can head north from there for a day at Matsushima Bay. Dotted with some 250 small grey-rock islands that are tufted by red and black pines, the bay is ranked as one of the top three scenic sites in Japan (As you may have noticed, Japan has rankings for almost everything!), and it's beautiful both from the boat tours that cruise the bay and the hills overlooking it. Or, there's an easy day trip inland to the mountain-top temple Yamadera, which is reached by a steep hour-long walk through ancient forest that's peppered with moss-covered statues. Not only is the site of Yamadera's Nokyodo and Kaisando buildings perched atop a cliff one of Tohoku's most impressive views, Yamadera is also one of the most memorable locations in haiku master Matsuo Basho's famous poem-filled travelogue around the Tohoku region, *The Narrow Road to the Deep North*, where in 1689 he wrote the classic haiku, "ah this silence / sinking into the rocks / voice of cicada."

ABOVE *Gyu-tan* (beef tongue) is one of Sendai's specialties. It gets served in several ways, but simple is best: grilled and dipped in freshly squeezed (and peppered) lemon juice.
TOP Matsushima Bay, just north of Sendai, is rated as one of Japan's most scenic spots.
LEFT Sendai's oldest celebration is the Aoba Matsuri, held on the third weekend in May. Performances include the famed Sparrow Dance.
RIGHT CENTER Cherry blossom picnics in central Sendai.
RIGHT The Naruko Gorge, 43 miles (70 kilometers) from Sendai, is in Naruko Onsen, an area known for its hot springs and ryokan.

ABOVE, LEFT AND BELOW
The spectacular mountain-top Yamadera shrine in Yamagata, reached by a steep hour-long walk through ancient forest.

ABOVE AND LEFT The World Heritage Chusonji Temple complex in Hiraizumi.
BELOW One of the three most important festivals in Tohoku is the summer Aomori Nebuta Festival, featuring floats with warrior figures.

Another option from Sendai is to head even further north. You could visit the rural surrounds of the Tono Valley, cycling around the farmland and learning about the area's rich folklore—with tales that range from mythical *kappa* (river imps), who drag children into ponds to oddities like the farmer's daughter who eloped with a horse—or check out the small town of Hiraizumi in Iwate Prefecture, which under the control of the Fujiwara clan in the eleventh and twelfth centuries was the effective center of the Tohoku region. With the World Heritage-listed Chusonji Temple in particular, the Fujiwaras left a stunning legacy in the town. Decorated gold and silver inside and out, it's a stark contrast to the hushed ancient forests surrounding it.

Or, go all the way to Aomori in the far north. Cold and in places wild, with a beautiful and rugged coastline that offers up fine, fresh seafood, Aomori is also home to Hirosaki and its magnificent castle: a three-story tower now designated as an Important Cultural Property, protected by a triple moat, which is pretty any time of year but especially so when the harsh northern winter finally departs and the cherry blossoms bloom in spring.

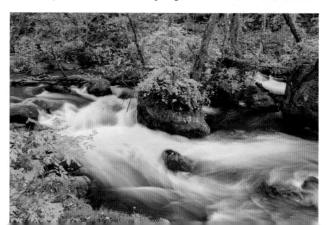

LEFT The Oirase River, which comes from Lake Towada. Beautiful year round, it's also considered one of Tohoku's most attractive fall destinations.

ABOVE The Aomori city skyline. The city itself isn't very built up, but the waterfront gives this otherwise low-key regional capital a cosmopolitan moment. The pyramid-shaped building is also worth visiting as it houses several good restaurants specializing in regional dishes.

LEFT Grilled seafood in Aomori. Besides seafood, this part of Japan is also known for its apples and hearty local dishes such as *jappa-jiru* hot pot (which uses every bit of a cod) and *kenoshiro*, a veg-packed miso soup.

LEFT Rice field art in Aomori. Several of the northern rice growing areas have artistic displays like this, which come into their own in summer and are created by planting various varieties and colors of rice plant. This one shows a popular Sunday night TV cartoon called *Sazae-san*, but the imagery varies annually.
ABOVE Hirosaki Castle in Aomori is one of the north's finest cherry blossom sites.

Hokkaido—a Different Japan

Like Okinawa in the sub-tropical south, the chilly far north of Japan has a character all of its own that in many ways makes it feel removed from other parts of Japan. In Hokkaido's case, harsh winters have certainly helped to set it apart, but so too has its relative youth and a lingering sense of frontier spirit. Sapporo, despite being Japan's fifth most populated city with 1.9 million residents, was only settled by the Japanese 140 years ago; before then, Sapporo and Hokkaido were inhabited only by the indigenous Ainu, who for generations faced discrimination from "pure" Japanese.

Aside from the several months of the year when it's carpeted with a deep layer of snow, Sapporo is a lovely city to explore. In summer, it's warm and sunny, but mostly avoids the oppressive heat and humidity of the rest of Japan. Better yet, it misses out on the muggy rainy season in June altogether. In spring and autumn, the city is fresh and full of color. It's also easy to get around, thanks to having been laid out in a grid system (unusual in Japan) at the center of which is a long green belt of park called Odori Koen. In summer, the park is the site of beer gardens and an internationally acclaimed outdoor jazz festival, while in February it becomes the main venue for the world-renowned Sapporo Snow Festival, when two million visitors descend on the city for an outdoor gallery of giant snow and ice sculptures.

For the Japanese, Sapporo is also known for its food—with signature dishes like a local version of ramen that uses a hearty miso-based broth, a cook-at-the table mutton barbecue named after Genghis Khan and warming soup curry, which is close to a mulligatawny soup. That's not to mention all the super fresh seafood that includes an array of crabs and some of the most consistently excellent sushi in Japan. To the south of Odori Koen, the restaurants and bars around the Tanukikoji shopping arcade are a great place to seek out local Sapporo flavors, as is the Susukino district, which despite its reputation for sleazy adult venues and pricey hostess clubs, also bursts with legitimate restaurants and bars and is something of a mecca for ramen fans in the shape of Ramen Yokocho, a covered alley

ABOVE Sapporo TV Tower in the central Odori Park is one of the city's most recognized landmarks.
TOP RIGHT Odori Park in central Sapporo.
MIDDLE RIGHT When in Sapporo or Otaru (or anywhere near the ocean in Hokkaido), don't miss the sushi. It's super fresh, cheaper than down south, and simply superb in quality.

ABOVE, TOP RIGHT AND MIDDLE RIGHT Sapporo Beer was one of the first European-influenced brews to turn sake drinkers into beer lovers. Japan now has dozens upon dozens of great craft brewers with arguably much better beer, but a visit to Sapporo should still include a pint of Sapporo just to say *kampai* (cheers!) for getting it all started here. **BELOW** The annual Yuki Matsuri (Snow Festival), Sapporo's largest event, sees the city transformed into an outdoor ice sculpture gallery.

RIGHT Sapporo ramen uses miso in the stock and slightly chewy noodles to give Hokkaido its distinctive take on the nation's favorite noodle. **BOTTOM RIGHT** Say "Hokkaido food" to many Japanese and they'll say *kani* (crab). Boiled, grilled, raw or however it comes, Hokkaido's numerous crab species are simply outstanding.

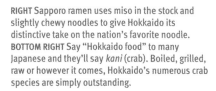

ABOVE, MIDDLE AND RIGHT The Ainu are northern Japan's indigenous people and their language has given Hokkaido many of its lovely place names. Discriminated against for generations for not being "pure Japanese",

things thankfully are far different now, and a visit to the Batchelor Kinenkan in Sapporo (above right) or a day trip to the Ainu Kotan Village (shown above) near Lake Akan provides the opportunity to learn about Ainu crafts and traditions.

BELOW LEFT The Otaru Canal and its old warehouses. **BOTTOM** Try Hokkaido specialties at a local restaurant that might include *Ishikari-nabe*, which uses the whole salmon, stewed with vegetables and tofu in miso-flavored kelp stock.
OPPOSITE PAGE, TOP AND MIDDLE Jozankei Onsen. Located in Shikotsu-Toya National Park, natural hot-spring waters were discovered here in 1866, sparking the development of ryokan (inns) and *onsen* baths. For a relaxed, traditional weekend away from Sapporo, Jozankei is popular, especially when the fall colors transform the town (top) and during the Yukitoro Snow Festival (bottom) in February.

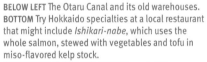

thick with the aroma of simmering chicken and pig bones and home to at least a dozen small ramen shops.

Head in other directions from Odori Koen and there are plenty of other well-known attractions nearby. At the park's eastern end, the 295-foot (90-meter) observation deck of the landmark TV Tower is a favorite for its views over the city and to the mountains beyond. A short walk north of the park comes a selection of Sapporo's historic sights, most notably the now iconic red brick building of the Former Hokkaido Government Office (a 1911 restoration of the late-1800s original) and the Hokkaido University Botanical Gardens, which are home to five thousand different types of Hokkaido flora and fauna

as well as the Batchelor Kinenkan, a museum dedicated to Hokkaido's indigenous Ainu people, with a small but excellent collection of artifacts.

Sapporo also makes a good base for exploring further afield. To the southwest is the hot-spring area of Jozankei, ideal for a good soak in piping hot natural waters and perhaps a night in a ryokan. But there is no day trip more popular than the 30-minute train ride north of central Sapporo to the harbor town of Otaru, which provides a glimpse of Hokkaido's early development, with its pretty cobbled streets and a canal that catches the reflections of nineteenth and early twentieth century stone buildings—now filled with restaurants and shops, but originally warehouses from

when Otaru boomed on the back of herring fishing and had a commercial district nicknamed "the Wall Street of the North". Nowadays, tourism and crafts are the main industries, Otaru especially being known for its glasswork and, like the rest of coastal Hokkaido, the quality of its seafood.

World-Class Skiing and Stunning Volcanic Landscapes

The best powder snow in the world, incredible natural beauty and the development of world-class resorts with a variety of accommodation options have made Niseko, 62 miles (100 kilometers) from Sapporo, the coolest (pardon the horrendous pun) winter destination in Asia over the past decade. For many Japanese skiers and boarders, not to mention Australians, Singaporeans, Koreans, Thais, and many others in Asia-Pacific, Niseko's slopes and backcountry have become an annual winter sports pilgrimage.

ABOVE The quality of the powder snow in Niseko attracts not just winter sports enthusiasts from across Japan, but from around Asia and Australasia.
LEFT Mount Yotei is one of the two main mountains that define Niseko and is referred to by locals as a smaller replica of Mount Fuji.
TOP RIGHT Night skiing and snowboarding at the Grand Hirafu resort in Niseko.

Niseko is defined by two mountains, the 6,227-foot (1,898-meter) Mount Yotei, often hidden in cloud yet still likened to Mount Fuji because of its symmetry, and the 4,291-foot (1,308-meter) Mount Niseko-Annupuri, which is home to the area's resorts and slopes. It's the latter that has given the area its name, and like many place names derived from the ethnic Ainu language of Hokkaido, it's wonderfully descriptive, translated to the rambling, but accurate, "mountain with a river, which runs around the bottom of a sheer cliff".

At the bottom of that mountain nowadays, running up its slopes, are a collection of four interconnected ski resorts—Grand Hirafu, Hanazono, Niseko Village, and Annupuri—that between them have every level of skier and snowboarder catered for, and (unusually for Japan) in a number of languages during a season that runs from approximately late November through to early May.

Niseko, however, isn't just a winter destination. Year-round, Niseko is known for its natural hot springs, the water of which is channeled into large communal

LEFT Niseko's resorts provide great skiing and boarding opportunities for all levels, but for the more experienced the area also has ample backcountry challenges.
RIGHT Hakodate has many old buildings that recall its earliest days and the Western influences of the Meiji era. The old warehouses by Hakodate's port, one of the first of Japan's ports to reopen to the rest of the world in the 1860s after centuries of self-imposed isolation, are now home to a collection of restaurants, bars and shops.

baths at many of the area's hotels and inns (and private open-air baths at some of the plushest ryokan), and which as well as relaxing and soothing the muscles and mind is said to alleviate all sorts of ailments. In spring and summer the area also offers up hiking trails, white-water rafting, canoeing, climbing, and other outdoor activities against a beautiful natural backdrop of flower-carpeted fields, lush green hills and rolling farmland.

Move on to the Oshima Peninsula in the far southwest of Hokkaido, and there are equally stunning sights in the town of Hakodate, where the night view over the city from Mount Hakodate is considered one of Japan's finest. Beyond that, the town itself—which is a direct bullet-train ride from Tokyo in about four hours on the Hayabusa—has a charm all of its own thanks to numerous remnants of its (and Hokkaido's) initial settlement. The Goryokaku Fort, built in the 1860s to help defend the newly settled area, is now a pleasant park area with intriguing star-shaped walls, while a walk around the city reveals a collection of Western-style

buildings, which include old British and Russian consulates as well as Russian Orthodox, Catholic and Episcopal churches. In a similar vein to Otaru, there are old warehouses here, too, now renovated into malls filled with shops and restaurants.

BELOW The Hakodate night view is one of the most famous sights in Japan, but the town's old Goryokaku Fort looks pretty impressive from above, too. It was built in the early settlement days to protect the new frontier, but now functions as parkland.

East from Sapporo into the Wild Hokkaido Hinterland

When you reach eastern Hokkaido, you discover Japan at its most rugged; you find nature untamed. Heading east away from Sapporo, it begins with sights like the stunning lavender fields of Furano and the rolling farmland of Tokachi, and then wilderness takes over. By the time you get to the far east, on the Shiretoko Peninsula, even a highly developed nation like Japan can say it is still unexplored.

The Kushiro area, to the southeast of Sapporo begins the journey into the wilderness. Here, Lake Akan, formed by volcanic activity six thousand years ago that has also given the area numerous hot springs, is one of Japan's most beautiful caldera lakes, with startlingly high water visibility and a peculiar type of algae called *marimo*, which forms into vivid green balls that have been adopted as something of a local symbol—you'll see cute *marimo* cartoon characters on everything from t-shirts to key rings to cookies in the local souvenir stores. Kushiro's main claim to fame, however, is marshland. Protected under the Ramsar Convention on Wetlands, the 45,220 acres (183 square kilometers) of marshland is by far the largest in Japan, providing a habitat for two thousand varieties of plant and animal life, including the protected Japanese crane (aka red-crowned crane), and bringing in a steady number of tourists to the area—some leisurely "cruising" through on the

ABOVE En route from Sapporo to the rugged east, the flower fields around the town of Biei are one of Hokkaido's most visited summer attractions. At the same time of year, the nearby town of Furano is carpeted with lavender.
LEFT Kushiro Port.
RIGHT Kushiro's Washo Market, located at the port, brings together sixty or so stalls selling freshly landed seafood that includes much of Japan's finest crab.
BELOW The blue king crab is a rare species that's found on the eastern tip of Hokkaido, around Nemuro. It has a rich taste and is often used in *nabe* hot pots.

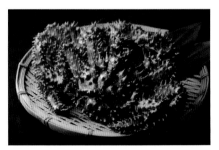

ABOVE To the northeast of Furano, just before the town of Biei, stop by at Shikisai-no-Oka to see the glorious flower gardens, which feature several different species of flora, including the lupine.

BELOW Endangered red-crowned cranes are the symbol of the Akan area, and a trip to the Akan International Crane Center (to learn about the artificial breeding efforts and more) is a must.

Norokko sightseeing train, others opting for more adventurous hot-air balloon rides over the wetlands or taking in the views from a canoe or on horseback.

Thick with virgin forest punctuated by sharp mountain peaks and a collection of five lakes, the whole Shiretoko Peninsula to the north east of Kushiro is designated as both a national park and listed as a UNESCO Natural Heritage Site, protecting its status as a habitat for not just a variety of bears and Sika deer, but bird life like Blackstone's fish owls and white-tailed sea eagles, which in winter can be seen soaring over the ice floes that speckle the Okhotsk Sea. The finely balanced underwater ecosystem is also the seasonal habitat for an incredible range of sea life, from sperm whales, mink whales and endangered fin whales to Dall's porpoises, making Shiretoko an invaluable natural resource.

RIGHT The Kamuiwakka Falls is a natural hot spring in Shiretoko National Park. Due to the danger of falling rocks, only the 460-foot (140-meter) lower section of the river is open to the public.

LEFT From January, the drift ice that moves south to Shiretoko is a major draw. Ice breakers take tourists on cruises through it, and you can even don special wetsuits and float with it. **RIGHT** One of the best places to see the Sika deer in Japan is at the Shiretoko National Park, a UNESCO World Heritage Site.

BELOW Located near the town of Rausu, this hot spring Kumanoyu (or literally, the Bear Hot Spring) has a mixed open-air bath and one for women.

BELOW RIGHT Steller's sea eagles, weighing in at up to 20 pounds (nine kilograms) and with distinctive yellow beaks, are one of Shiretoko's most striking inhabitants. In winter, they hunt Pacific cod through gaps in the drift ice and can be watched from shore or icebreaker tours.

FAR LEFT Hokkaido is bear country. You see bear warning signs in many parts of the island (and bears appear on lots of the souvenirs), but in Shiretoko you can actually go and watch them in their natural habitat.
BACK ENDPAPER Ginkakuji in Kyoto in autumn.

Photo Credits

Published by Tuttle Publishing, an imprint of Periplus Editions (HK) Ltd

www.tuttlepublishing.com

Copyright © 2017 Periplus Edition (HK) Ltd

ISBN: 978-4-8053-1388-6
LCC No: 2016955490

Distributed by

North America, Latin America & Europe
Tuttle Publishing
364 Innovation Drive, North Clarendon, VT 05759-9436 USA
Tel: 1 (802) 773-8930; Fax: 1 (802) 773-6993
info@tuttlepublishing.com; www.tuttlepublishing.com

Japan
Tuttle Publishing
Yaekari Building, 3rd Floor, 5-4-12 Osaki, Shinagawa-ku, Tokyo 141-0032
Tel: (81) 3 5437-0171; Fax: (81) 3 5437-0755
sales@tuttle.co.jp; www.tuttle.co.jp

Asia Pacific
Berkeley Books Pte Ltd
3 Kallang Sector, #04-01/02, Singapore 349278
Tel: (65) 6280-1330; Fax: (65) 6280-6290
inquiries@periplus.com.sg; www.periplus.com

21 20 19 18   6 5 4 3 2

Printed in Hong Kong   1810EP

Acknowledgments

First and foremost, thanks to the English and Japanese sides of my
family, stretching from Devon and Cornwall to Tokyo and beyond,
for their love and support in everything I do. More than anything,
love to my wife Yoko and son Arthur. I'm fortunate to travel to many
amazing places for work—and I hope people who read this book will
be inspired to visit many of them, too—but the journey home will
always be my favorite because of them.

About Tuttle
"Books to Span the East and West"

Our core mission at Tuttle Publishing is to create books
which bring people together one page at a time. Tuttle was
founded in 1832 in the small New England town of Rutland,
Vermont (USA). Our fundamental values remain as strong
today as they were then—to publish best-in-class books
informing the English-speaking world about the countries
and peoples of Asia. The world has become a smaller place
today and Asia's economic, cultural and political influence
has expanded, yet the need for meaningful dialogue and
information about this diverse region has never been
greater. Since 1948, Tuttle has been a leader in publishing
books on the cultures, arts, cuisines, languages and
literatures of Asia. Our authors and photographers have
won numerous awards and Tuttle has published thousands
of books on subjects ranging from martial arts to paper
crafts. We welcome you to explore the wealth of information
available on Asia at **www.tuttlepublishing.com**.